THE OTHER SIDE OF LIFE

THE OTHER SIDE OF LIFE

OVER 60?
GOD STILL HAS A PLAN FOR YOU!

REV. WARREN C. BIEBEL JR.

Healthy Life Press
Orlando, Florida

THE OTHER SIDE OF LIFE:
OVER 60? GOD STILL HAS A PLAN FOR YOU!

Copyright © 2010, 2013 by Rev. Warren C. Biebel Jr., and Healthy Life Press, 2603 Drake Drive, Orlando, FL 32810

www.healthylifepress.com

Cover design by Judy Johnson

Printed in the United States of America

All rights reserved. No part of this publication may be reproduced, stored in a retrieval system, or transmitted in any form or by any means – for example, electronic, photocopy, recording – without the prior written permission of the publisher. The only exception is brief quotations in printed reviews. Undesignated biblical references are from the King James version of the Bible. Other versions used are indicated in text.

Library of Congress Cataloging-in-Publication Data

Biebel, Warren C., Jr.
The Other Side of Life: Over 60? God Still Has a Plan for You!

ISBN 978-1-9392-6734-4

1. Aging; 2. Christian Living For Seniors

Most Healthy Life Press resources are available worldwide through bookstores and online outlets, depending on their format. This book also exists in a downloadable and printable PDF from www.healthylifepress.com. Multiple copy discounts available from the publisher at the address above, or by e-mail: info@healthylifepress.com. Copying or redistributing printed or eBook formatted books or portions thereof is a violation of international copyright law.

Dedication

Through many years, it has been my privilege to share my life with a multitude of special people. My wonderful family and dear friends have blessed me with encouragement and love. Others have crossed my path, some for different periods of time, and many much too briefly.

When it is all added up, it is these good people who have filled my life with excitement, pleasure, and just plain fun. Yet, the ingredient that made the journey complete was God's presence in it all. When, as a teenager, Jesus came into my heart and life, He brought a kind of love for others I had not, or could not, have known.

I would like to dedicate my book to all of those who made life for me not only worth living, but also blessed and satisfying.

Thanks especially to my very special wife, Marian, and to my son, Dave, for rekindling my interest in completing this book, which I started to write so many years ago.

Acknowledgements

I wish to thank Judy B. Johnson, our cover creator, her sister, Lori B. Noonkester, and their mother, Francis C. Branson, for acting as our models for the cover.

Francis C. Branson authored the poem on page eight, entitled "The Strange Reflection," which she has allowed us to use here.

Publisher's Note:

In order to enhance the practical use of this book for both personal study and use in a group setting, this updated edition includes chapter-specific questions for personal reflection and/or group duscussion in the Appendix, which starts on page 141. These questions are best viewed by the individual reader or group discussion leader as tools whose purpose is to enhance understanding of each chapter's topic, and not as a task that the reader or study group must try to finish within any particular timeframe; for example, within the span of a one-hour meeting. We invite your feedback and suggestions regarding additions or changes that might improve this section. E-mail these to: info@healthylifepress.com, or mail them to Healthy Life Press; 2603 Drake Drive; Orlando, FL 32810. Thank you.

FOREWORD

by Sharon V. King, PhD – Sociologist/Gerontologist; Author of
The Spiritual Fitness Checkup For The 50-Something Woman
(Healthy Life Press, 2010)

Books about religion and aging have grown in popularity as the "greying of America" impacts church congregations and clergy. Few approach the topic of the role of religion in later life as meaningfully as *The Other Side of Life* by Rev. Warren C. Biebel Jr.

Drawing on biblical examples and his 60-plus years of pastoral experience, Rev. Biebel helps older (and younger) adults understand God's view of aging and the rich life available to everyone who seeks a deeper relationship with God as they age.

Rev. Biebel explains how to:

◆ Identify God's ongoing plan for your life

◆ Rely on faith to manage the anxieties of aging

◆ Form positive, supportive relationships

◆ Cultivate patience

◆ Cope with new technologies

◆ Develop spiritual integrity

◆ Understand the effects of dementia

◆ How to develop a Christ-centered perspective of aging

I highly recommend this book for readers of all ages, but especially for those on the 60-plus side of life.

The Strange Reflection

Today I saw a stranger,
She looked a lot like me.
At first I thought I knew her,
So I stepped real close to see.
"I've seen those eyes before," I said,
"But can't remember where.
The girl that I mistook you for
Has long and dark brown hair.
I see you've earned a silver crown,"
I told the stranger then.
She replied, "I've worn this crown
Since . . . I can't remember when."
The stranger smiled. 'Twas then I saw
The wrinkles 'round her eyes.
Something else I noticed, too:
The difference in our size.
I turned to walk away from her,
This stranger I'd just met,
But something made me look again;
We're so alike . . . and yet . . .
"Can you be me? The real true me?
If so, then who am I?"
"You don't exist," the stranger said,
"A mirror cannot lie."

Francis Branson
10-29-91

INTRODUCTION

As I approached and then entered the preliminary phases of my retirement years, I began to personally encounter many new and complex thoughts. These involved my past life, preparations and problems related to the changing of roles, and a hard look into the future.

These musings also included my observations about friends involved in the same experiences. I became profoundly aware that decisions made during pre-retirement and early retirement, and even into later years, can lead to either happiness and satisfaction or a sense of futility and tragedy. In the following pages, I have tried to express in Christian terms my own feelings, and to interpret them in a way that will help others.

The book takes us through a variety of ideas and observations, all related to looking at life as it confronts seniors today. Woven throughout is the idea of the continuing plan of God and His desire to use us, regardless of our age. It deals with issues that are of the greatest concern to older people, while relating the solutions to these concerns to the Bible and our Christian faith.

Some of these issues are:

❖ The need to take the time and make the effort to see where we have been, where we are now, and where we are headed

❖ The willingness to see ourselves as important in God's plan to reach the world, and particularly young people, for Christ. We are a vital link to the past, and thus a bridge to the future for those coming along behind us

❖ The importance of facing and dealing with our anxieties squarely, since these can rob our joy and block our happiness day by day

❖ The conviction that personal integrity in our relationship with

God and others is of paramount importance

❖ The realization that all around us, people are suffering with various types of mental illness, and we can show them the compassion that Jesus would show them if He were here - for indeed, He is here, living in and through His followers

❖ The commitment to trying to bring together the divided Body of Christ, and to tell the truth to young people about the cost of living for Christ. Only the wisdom that comes with age and experience can accomplish these things.

As I look back, I see a long, remarkable, sometimes wondrous and sometimes very difficult journey that is called "life." I started collecting my thoughts for this book nearly two decades ago, when I thought that age sixty was a significant mile marker on my way toward reunion with many loved ones who had already gone before me. Now that I'm eighty-something, I've come to see some of the issues in this book a little differently, yet most have been confirmed by observation and experience as the world, and our culture, has "evolved" or "devolved" – sometimes it's not that easy to say which is the best description of where we've been going.

Nevertheless, this one thing I do know. Neither God nor His principles found in His Word have changed one bit; in fact, they're more relevant and needful now than they were twenty years ago, for only they can provide that "anchor for the soul" that all of us, young or old, need.

A few years ago, I tried to capture this sentiment in the following poem:

GOD SPOKE – I ANSWERED

The special wonders of this world and the universe are all around us.

God's Hand of creation is glorious and is there to be seen and shared by all.

To those who cannot, or will not see, I say "Open your eyes and hearts to such a great God!"

Out of the untold millions throughout history and also today, He came to me one day and said, "Come" and I came to Him.

What a great life it has been with warm friendships, thrilling experiences, singing, playing, working but best of all, a quiet walk with Him.

Sometimes, in the sunlight, a few times in the shadows, but always with Him in my heart.

But there is a better place and one that can be reached. It is a special place where Jesus is, and whatever else it has, that is enough. To be there with Him.

I can say good-bye to all this great world has offered me because there will be a hello when the time comes.

It will be my Savior saying, "Come" once again and I will answer "I come."

by Warren C. Biebel Jr. - 4/21/2009

Contents

CHAPTER 1 Going South in the Northbound Lane 15

CHAPTER 2 A Bridge Over Troubled Waters 31

CHAPTER 3 If the Ship Leaks, Is it Sinking? 43

CHAPTER 4 Don't Throw that Club! 49

CHAPTER 5 Bank Accounts, IOUs, Bouncing Checks 55

CHAPTER 6 Bells, Buzzers, and Whistles 61

CHAPTER 7 Doing Business in Great Waters – Dealing with Current Events 69

CHAPTER 8 Thunder and Lightning 85

CHAPTER 9 Unitarians, Fire, and Personal Integrity 89

CHAPTER 10 The Other Side of the Other Side of life 109

CHAPTER 11 Skyhooks, Snipes, and Left-handed Monkey Wrenches 125

CONCLUSION:
From Perception to Reality - Our Journey Through Life 131

Questions for Personal Reflection and/or Group Discussion 141

Healthy Life Press Resources 154

1

GOING SOUTH IN THE NORTHBOUND LANE

It is very early on a Sunday morning in October - one of those special days in Northern New England when the crisp air and the spectacular colors make life effervescent. I am headed north on Interstate 91 out of Windsor Vermont toward White River Junction. It's hard to keep from singing to myself on a day like this and the semi-deserted highway provides an excellent forum for reflecting on life. In a few minutes I will be conducting a worship service at the Veterans' Hospital where I am the Protestant chaplain.

As I come over the crest of a hill and begin the long downgrade, a panoramic view opens up before me. To the north and west lie the green rolling hills of Vermont, resplendent in their festive fall colors. Below me and to the east lies the wide Connecticut River, its mirror-water reflecting the red and golden hues of autumn. What an idyllic scene, and I am part of it!

At that precise moment, I am startled to see another vehicle - a car proceeding toward me in my lane, a car coming south in the northbound lane of the interstate highway, and we are closing fast! Shaken out of my fantasy world, I know that the situation calls for immediate action and I quickly assess the surroundings. Looking in the mirror, I am thankful that there are no eighteen wheelers barreling down behind me. My next reaction is to begin blinking my headlights in a rather hostile manner at the approaching vehicle. Apparently, the driver gets my message because, as we draw nearer, he begins to slow down.

As we come upon each other, we come to a complete stop,

side by side, in the middle of the northbound lane. The window of the other car opens revealing a middle aged man, dressed in a Sunday suit and wearing a broad brimmed hat. "Is this the way to Boston?" he asks in a somewhat shaky voice. My answer is very firm and quite prophetic: "If you don't get out of this lane, you'll never make it! You're in the wrong lane - hurry up and cross over to the southbound!"

There is a sudden screeching of tires as the message gets through. With one of the quickest U-turn maneuvers ever attempted and in a cloud of dust, leaves, and smoke, he is gone!

I have reflected on that incident many times in the succeeding years. A man in middle age in the wrong lane, heading for certain destruction, unless he changed his direction! It's a perfect picture of life, as Proverbs 14:12 says, "There is a way which seemeth right unto a man, but the ends thereof are the ways of death."

This illustration is appropriate to the thesis of this book, *The Other Side of Life*. As we approach the other side of life - our retirement years, which lane are we in? Are we just going where life seems to lead, letting the "car" take us, or are we in control? Are we headed in the right direction? Did we heed the warning signs or did we miss them altogether? Is there anything we can do about it?

Above all, we need to take a look at ourselves! What do you see when you look in the mirror? After sixty-plus years, some see a person they thought would never exist; a wrinkled, white-haired, tired individual, ever growing more dependent and insecure. Others see an attractive, dynamic person, competent and self-assured. For the one, life has become a struggle for survival. For the other, life is still expanding, holding promise of new challenges and opportunities. What makes the difference? That is what this book is about.

First we need to make an appraisal - something we should have done a long time ago, but most likely didn't. For some reason, age has a way of creeping up on us. At forty and then fifty, we were still planning big events in our life - then suddenly we hit sixty and life took on an entirely different aura. We went through all those years without thinking about what it would be like to be on the "other side of life."

A professional property appraiser studies an old house from every perspective: the condition of the structure itself; repairs that are needed; it's desirability and location; and, the furnishings. When we appraise ourselves to discover where we are now, where we have been and where we are going, we must be honest.

Comparing ourselves to a house being appraised is not unusual, for Jesus compared life itself to the building of a house, among other things. He taught that the building should be built on solid rock, that we should count the cost, and that we should be careful to use good materials.

He began with the foundation, and this is a good way to start our self-appraisal. Is your life after sixty built on a solid foundation? Rest assured that it is if you have a living faith in Jesus Christ and follow the trustworthy blueprint in the Word of God. If, on the other hand, you have neglected the spiritual side of life, in those earlier years, later, when the inevitable storms gather and begin to beat upon you, your "house" cannot stand. In any case, it's never too late to gain a new perspective and welcome a vital and living faith. That will be your foundation for the years ahead.

And what about the structural condition of your house? Is it a little worn, weather-beaten, in need of repair? Are some of its parts beyond repair? Is it attractive to look at, and does it have a warm, friendly, beckoning atmosphere in spite of being somewhat weather-beaten? We'll be dealing with these questions in more detail later. Suffice it to say, now, that we need to take a long, hard, honest look at ourselves. It is of the utmost importance that, if our goal with this appraisal is to make the remaining years of our lives as satisfying and successful as possible, we must have a 100 percent true picture of what we were and who we are now. But what if what we see frightens us?

Let's try to answer that. The concept of God having a personal plan for our lives permeates the whole Bible. From Abraham's servant finding a wife for Isaac, to Jesus meeting the woman at the well, there is always that personal touch. Most Christians believe in that personal daily touch of God, but, for some reason, many seem to believe that that "plan" ends for them between fifty-five and sixty-five years of age.

One of the most inspirational stories of the Old Testament concerns Caleb, the old "bulldog" who was promised a mountaintop of property as a young spy, after going into the land of Canaan with Joshua. When circumstances finally permitted, Caleb came, being more than eighty years old, to claim his land for himself and his family. It's that kind of "hanging in there" spirit that more of us need because it is a winning spirit. The beginning of the end for us is when we lose the motivation to enhance our lives with new ideas and growth. There is absolutely no biblical or other reason to think that God's special plan for our individual lives ends at a particular age, or for that matter, ever.

If a person enters the "after sixty" stage of life with a firm belief that God has a will and plan for his or her life, this provides a firm foundation for all of the other considerations. But it is important for us not to confuse God's will for ours. I may have made extensive plans for my retirement but they may not work out. In fact, very few plans work out exactly as we envisioned. That is because we do not have access to future elements that will help shape the plan. However, I strongly recommend something that many "seniors" have not done and that is to sit down at a quiet, relaxed time with your spouse, or by yourself, if you are single, and after seeking God's guidance, actually put down on paper the specifics of your plan for the coming years.

God deals with "ingredients." His plan is never a series of unconnected events! During my college days, I once heard a speaker challenge us as students to consider a missionary career. His message was inspiring, but when he came to the part concerning how to determine where to go as a missionary, his message came apart. His idea was that we should get a large world map, spread it out on the floor, pray for help, close our eyes, and point to a particular geographical location. That would be the place where God had called us for a life ministry. This is the Ouija board mentality of some Christians. But it is definitely not biblical!

Ridiculous as this may seem, there are many older adults who are making the important and oftentimes life-altering decisions on just such flimsy, unscriptural ideas. The Christian life, while guided and directed by the Holy Spirit, is not one decided by spiritual voodoo or black magic. His Word is still the "lamp" to our feet for the short run and a "searchlight" to our path for the longer term. God for the most part, deals with circumstances and what I call "ingredients." It is as we consider these that we find His will and plan.

It was our privilege to found and operate a Christian conference and retreat center for a number of years. It is set among the beautiful hills of New Hampshire and provides a glorious environment for spiritual renewal. Many of our guests have had a "mountaintop" experience while there. Over the years, numerous individuals have come to me and said something like this: "The Lord has told me to work here. Do you have an opening?"

My problem is trying to encourage them to seek God's will for service while explaining to them the realities of life in our setting and particularly of the hard work required to keep things going. Their problem is to separate emotions and desires from isolated incidents. God almost always works in an "ordered" plan, a progression of events and experiences leading up to important life altering decisions. While I have never said "no" directly to these well-meaning folks, I have explained the work load, the poor pay scale, and the pitfalls, along with the rewards of working in a Christian environment. Of all those who have claimed to hear the voice of God calling them to work with us, not one has ever followed through!

One thing is certain, God does have a continuing plan for "seniors." That should be evident from the fact that every time one of His biblical servants of old tried to use age as an excuse, the Lord had to correct him. Elijah is perhaps the best example. Old and tired and worn out from his battles with Jezebel and the prophets of Baal, he wanted to throw in the towel. A loving God encouraged and strengthened him, but He also said that Elijah still had a job to do. And he went on to do it! Then when he was finished, God took him home.

Another thing that is certain is that while God's plan continues to contain pleasing, exciting, satisfying elements, it also encompasses the other more distressing side of life.

One of the most important proofs of the truth of the whole gospel account of Jesus is contained in what He said and did not say. Had He been a counterfeit or an imposter, He would not have told "truths" that hurt. He would not have said such things as "in the world you will have tribulations." Have you ever known a politician who was seeking adherents to say such things as Jesus said? If you were trying to build a new religion in a world where political leaders and tyrants always covered up their defeats, would you confront your potential followers with teachings such as Jesus did? "Good time" preachers of today notwithstanding, we must include in our thinking and plans the possibilities, probabilities, and actuality of unpleasant and downright difficult events.

The nuclear industry now has a phrase used to define a dangerous incident at a facility - they call it an "unusual event." While we as "senior" Christians will sometimes have to deal with sudden emergency events, they will not be "unusual" in the sense that they happen outside the plan of God. In one way, it would be glorious if we never had to deal with the loss of a loved one or the incapacity of a friend, a financial disaster, or even our own illness or death, but we are not taught, either by Jesus Himself or any of the Scriptures, that we are exempt from those events which are part of the nature of the world and of man. What we are taught is that we will have, and in fact do have now, perhaps lying latent within us, the power and presence of God giving us strength to deal with any and all testings.

1 Corinthians 10:12-13 says, "So if you think you are standing firm, be careful that you don't fall! No temptation has seized you, except what is common to man. And God is faithful. He will

not let you be tempted beyond what you can bear. But when you are tempted (tested), He will also provide a way out so that you can stand up under it."

Beyond that, we have the promise that ours will be a continuing and growing existence, not bound by the element of time as we know it now.

While we're thinking of the harder side of growing old, we need to ask ourselves some difficult questions. Are we prepared for the loss of long-time friends and family? Can we stand the inevitable inroads of wear and tear on our health? Perhaps the most significant question of all is: Can I deal with the loss experiences that seem senseless and unfair? It seems to me that in order to successfully handle these things, we must begin with an admission that we don't have a rational answer for them.

From my own personal experience, we have missionary friends who have lost children, Godly men and women gone with cancer, loved ones gone, some in the distant past, some still fresh in the memory, but none forgotten. To be the men and women that God wants us to be is to find a resolution to this basic problem. It is indeed a demanding commitment which says "we walk by faith and not by sight." The bottom line is this - we do not have all the answers, but we do have "THE ANSWER." We believe that all things do work together for good to those who love God and walk in His will, and we are assured that there will come a time when we will have access to all the answers. This is a far better alternative than to live out our years filled with bitterness, anger, and confusion. As for the future, God promises that one day we will know, not only the sequence of events, but the reasons for them.

1 Corinthians 13:12 says, "Now we see but a poor reflection; then we shall see face to face. Now I know in part; then shall I know fully even as I am known."

Now, on to the pleasing, exciting, and satisfying aspects of growing older with Christ. We'll get a really big surprise if we expect "retirement" to be a time of idleness. We have a small home in Florida in a neighborhood where most of the people are retired. Many of them are working hard, or harder than ever before, and the reason is quite simple. Life becomes an absolute zero if we do not get any satisfaction from what we are doing.

So my first suggestion concerning this phase of life is to stop calling it "retirement" and find a better, more descriptive word, such as the "great adventure," or perhaps the "Caleb club." But let's be sure we choose a name that incorporates the idea of living a life of excitement and fulfillment. I know of a church that has a group for those over sixty called the "Sunset Club." Would you like to be a member?

Whatever the name, the years ahead should include certain ingredients. At the very top I put "relationships," and I start with my wife, family, and friends. This time of life with its relative freedom from responsibility can be one of the happiest, most fulfilling of all. There's time to do some of the things you have hoped to do, like traveling, pursuing hobbies or special interests, taking care of your home, and of course, there are literally hundreds of other things to do. But of the greatest value are the warm relationships that you have built and can now enjoy. Pity those who never took the time. But it is not too late!

Remember, though, if you have relationships but forget "service" you'll be missing out on one of God's greatest gifts, the privilege to serve Him; the result will be lost opportunity.

As we grow older, we need what I call "mind sharpening" tools. These come in different forms such as books and newspapers, social activities, interest in current events, conversation, and communication with others. Yet the greatest tool of all is still the Bible, because it has the ability to renew your mind. When I was a pastor, one of the greatest ladies I knew was one of our church deaconesses who was in her early 90s at the time. She confided to me that she had forgotten much of the Bible that she had memorized as a younger woman, a natural result of advancing age. Her solution was simple - start memorizing again, and she did, first the Ten Commandments and then other appropriate Scriptures. Several years later as she prepared to die, her mind was clear and sharp and she was actually looking forward to being with the Lord.

There are some things that we can't control, such as the loss of memory, hearing, or sight, but we can do all in our power to maintain them. It will take work!

One of the basic decisions we have to make concerns our lifestyle. It is at this point that many older people make a tragic mistake. It is not necessary to go off the deep end in one direction or the other to be happy. There are those who try to reverse the aging process by living a super flamboyant "second childhood" life. Let's face it - after sixty I am not going to build my muscles by weight lifting, though it might help me to maintain the muscles I already have. In fact, there is little I can change about my body. The best I can hope for is a "holding action" and that is an important contribution to my well-being. So sports such as jogging, tennis, golf, and swimming or any other physical exertion within reason make a lot of sense. On the other hand, physical fanaticism will only produce much frustration in the long run.

Traveling down a certain road in Roseland, Florida, on any given day, you'll see an interesting sight - a slightly built woman attired in an outfit reminiscent of the knights of old. From head to toe, she is adorned with weights of every kind and metallic looking clothes designed to produce perspiration. She is walking at a fast pace, swinging her arms in perpetual motion in the hot Florida sun. In each hand are small weights. I give this woman a lot of credit for determination, but so far, at least, for all that torture she always appears, physically, exactly the same. We need to find the right proportion of exercise "ingredients" to add just the right seasoning to our life.

The Apostle Paul put it this way, "Bodily exercise profits a little, but godliness with contentment is great gain." This is true because in spite of all I may do to reinforce good health, there are things that can and do go wrong. Recently, we had a weekend retreat, and as part of the activities we had an "Old Fogies" softball game. Those of us of the over-sixty group amazed the younger set with our dexterity and power at the plate. The problem came with running the bases. Why, one of our "fogies" turned three solid home runs into singles! We came through it in good shape; however, as I was walking about the grounds later in the day, I stepped into a small indentation in the ground and wrenched my knee. Ever since then my knee makes a "clicking" sound. This illustrates how even minor accidents can affect our overall health.

It is important, as we grow older, that while we seek total honesty about ourselves we also temper our thinking with conscious and deliberate forgetfulness of age. Each day brings a different experience! Sometimes we wake up feeling like a teenager again, and sometimes we barely make it out of bed.

In either case, "mind control" is especially important to us since living on a certain "plane" is much more critical to our overall health than the mountain peak and valley syndrome that many seniors experience. We can avoid the depressions of "bad" days and the excesses of "good" days by combining a "fighting" spirit with one of calmness, thanksgiving, and commitment.

One of the things I have found to be most important, on a given day, is that even before I have a chance to fully analyze how I feel, in prayer I commit that day to the Lord with whatever it may hold. In that way, whether it proves to be a day of great pleasure or one of difficult testing, I'll be ready! My relationship to God will be reassuring and viable from the very beginning.

One side of "age fanaticism" is the fantasy world of superficial flamboyancy. The other side can be just as bad or worse. Let's call it ritualistic hocus pocus. In simpler terms it is the idea that you'll be happy and secure if every detail of your life is planned by you. This is a great deception, because God intended our lives to be interesting and exciting. He gave us the "pioneering" and "exploring" spirit. I think wealthy people have the greatest problem with this, but I am not sure why. Perhaps it's because poor and moderately wealthy people can find adventure in more menial things, for example, shopping at discount stores, or even just "window shopping" without buying anything.

My wife and I were once invited to spend several days in Miami, Florida, on a beautiful yacht - a sleek converted Corvette, it was one hundred fifteen feet long and had a crew of three. Now this was a bit incredulous for us, since we only had enough money to fly to Miami and back and a few dollars for spending. However, "our" yacht was berthed in the Miami Boatyard in between Jackie Gleason's four hundred foot yacht and another one on the other side. One afternoon, as we were sitting in the main cabin, a wealthy gentleman and his wife came aboard to discuss the purchase of a new boat.

Assuming that we were important people and while her husband was negotiating, the wife insisted that we accompany her to view their new eighty foot yacht. After viewing that glistening new boat with its great, master bedroom, including a king-sized bed, giant TV, and all other amenities, she proceeded to tell us what it was like to be so rich. Her husband was not satisfied with their new hacienda; in fact, he wasn't satisfied with anything. They had gone through numerous yachts and haciendas. That very afternoon, she would be attending an important art auction in downtown Miami. She had $25,000.00 to spend that day, and the particular piece was not important to her as long as it was in blue. The thought did cross my mind that I had a beautiful "blue" picture back home in New Hampshire that might be just right for her. My wife and I left, thinking how good God had been to us to let us be poor!

Some years ago I spent a summer on a very wealthy exclusive resort island on Cape Cod. I was there to tutor two young children who were spending the summer with their grandmother and a maid. The people living on this island were among the wealthiest in the world at that time. One of the most interesting things I observed about the social life of this group was that from the youngest children to the elder adults, a most important ritual was the planning well in advance of every miniscule detail of daily life. Last minute unforeseen change produced a sense of horror and a frantic race to "save" the day. In the search for "social security" these people were sacrificing such important ingredients of life as spontaneity and creativity in daily activities. While not quite as dramatic, many older people do just that in their concern for social "security," and the resulting "ritualism." To be happy, we do not need to have an all encompassing plan for every day. Of course, a general and sometimes more specific plan for special events is important, but not to the sacrificing of spontaneity and creativity. Once we have gone the "ritual" route, our lives will inevitably become boring, unimaginative, and unsatisfying.

The reaction to ritualism is bizarre behavior! Weekends at the "Cape" were like that. While I was not there, I heard stories of wild parties, climbing in and out of windows, drunkenness, and all kinds of reveling. Evidently this behavior had its effect upon the young boys and girls, because several years later I picked up a Boston paper and there to my horror on the front page was a picture of the little girl I had tutored in math and English, now grown up. She had shot and killed her mother's boyfriend as he entered their Beacon Hill apartment through a window.

I am convinced that wild and bizarre behavior is a product of an unhappy, unsatisfied lifestyle, a form of social rebellion. How important then, that we find in our life God's secret of contentment and demonstrate it to others. Ritualism can work its way into the most intimate areas of life. As a pastor, I once had a young wife come to me for counseling. She had a deep love for her older husband, but there was something missing in their "love" experience. This man had been brought up in a military home. Everything was done precisely as planned and on a tight schedule. Life was a military "ritual." Having been brought up that way, this man found that kind of living a satisfactory lifestyle for himself. In fact, he brought it with him into their bedroom affairs and sexual relationship. To him, the sexual experience became a twice a week ritual, on specific days and at a specific time, instead of it being a love affair. To her, this behavior lacked spontaneity and cast doubt on how real his love really was. It took away the deep, thrilling, sensitive meaning of sexual love and made it a military exercise.

Ritualism can extend to every area of life if we permit it to do so . . . and it will get worse as we grow older. Our circle of friends will grow smaller, and the experiences of life will grow less important and less meaningful. One way you can tell if ritualism is taking over your life is if you automatically sit in the same seat each Sunday in church. This is one of the biggest hang-ups for the pastor of a small to medium-sized church. To look out on the congregation every Sunday and see the same people in the same seats with the same expressions on their faces is not only disconcerting but downright demoralizing. Try to move them to a new location and if they will not move, it is guaranteed that they cannot be "moved" by the message, or even by the Spirit of God!

Let's not give in to ritualism. Let's keep the spirit of adventure in our lives but keep in mind that not every adventure has a successful ending. Some years ago, when we first moved to the country, my wife and I decided that rather than having the same old menu every week, we would try one new kind of food, at least once a week. Since I had taken up hunting as a hobby and because we were on a very limited budget. I confidently told her that I would bring home the "bacon" for our new food experiment. Venison proved to be a success even though to our taste it was rather dry and not as good as beef. However, as I triumphantly brought home first a rabbit and then a squirrel, our enthusiasm began to wane and the final blow came when we decided to splurge and buy a live lobster. Well, watching that animal cook in the boiling water with its eyes still open was too much for my wife. So much for the food adventure!

Still, we haven't let "ritualism" take over our lives and I thank God for it. A few years ago, some of our friends, knowing that we desperately needed a vacation, offered us the use of their condominium in Florida. For that first trip, we scratched together enough money for the trip and departed. We could have found a million excuses for not going, including finances, family, or work. What's more, we didn't even know if we would like Florida. Well, we've never been sorry. The Lord's good plan for our lives began unfolding as we found our trips to Florida were just what we New Hampshirites needed in order to recover from those long, hard winters. Our work demanded that we be in the North through the long, cold months. Later, God provided an opportunity through a small inheritance for us to buy a modest home in Florida for our annual treks south. This has opened many new vistas to us, including new friends, a new church, neighbors, and a home that offers us projects and improvement opportunities. All in all, it has added an exciting new dimension to our lives.

Variety of living does not diminish your present life. I believe that as you enlarge your horizons of living, your present relationships, whether family, friends, or your life work will be enhanced and more meaningful. Scripture encourages us in this regard. Isaiah 54:2-3 says, "Enlarge the place of your tent, stretch your tent curtains wide, do not hold back; lengthen your cords, strengthen your stakes. For you will spread out to the right and to the left."

When I think of lives of diminished happiness, a special lady who came into my career when I was a pastor comes to mind. From a purely factual point of view, life had not been particularly kind to her. Her husband had died of cancer and she had the constant care of living with her elderly mother and the confining aspect that had on her life. In addition, she had serious physical problems of her own to deal with. It was in this setting that we became acquainted and I became involved as a friend and counselor. I'll never forget that as we entered the new year, we talked and prayed over the telephone as we often did and she expressed to me her hope that the year ahead would be different and good for her. I assured her that as we accepted the promises of God's Word together, life could be much better. However, the Lord had a severe test in His plan for her first. It was discovered shortly thereafter that she had a brain tumor. What could I tell her? I had no special line to heaven to know what would happen. Was there a flaw in our plan of faith? After all, good friends and dedicated Christians had been taken with cancer and tumors. Was this going to happen to her?

Part of our commitment to Christ revolves around this very issue. How far does the promise of health, healing, and the continuation of life itself extend to us and to what degree should they affect our "faith commitment"? I have come to believe that the deepest sorrows, the most heart wrenching losses that come to believers, are not random, even though they are a part of the human, world experience.

It is not contradictory to say that God can spare a life but that He does not always do so. If we say that He always heals, that He always spares or "intervenes," we deceive ourselves, for there is no such promise. Had there been, Stephen would have continued his "faith ministry" as the first deacon and the many Christian men and women lost in war, accidents, illness, and tragedies would have lived on.

No, our problem is that we don't think as God does. He operates in a different time, space, and material existence than we do, one that we do not and cannot fully comprehend. His ways are not our ways and His thoughts are not our thoughts, though we do find His message in the Word of God. We are not living in the same eternal dimension. So acceptance of difficult, oftentimes heart wrenching events and experiences is not easy. The alternative though, is far worse. Our faith experience extends to the unknown and to the often hard reality of the known; if it doesn't, then it's a counterfeit.

Back to that special lady. It was discovered to our joy that her tumor was benign, and after successful surgery many of her other physically interconnected problems were cleared up. Later that year she met and married a fine man who had also lost his partner to illness. This experience portrays what I am trying to say about adventure, because this Christian couple enjoyed going to Florida for the winter where they found great enjoyment in their church and social life. One of their favorite activities was square dancing. This lady made it from the circumstances of drudgery and confinement to one of activity and happiness. Take the risks, launch out to a better, fuller life with the Lord. Beat the ritualism.

Remember though, never lose the basic premise that God has a special plan for your life right through to the end. Paul expressed it this way, "I have fought a good fight, I have finished my course, I have kept the faith and the time of my departure is near." I would like to think of it this way. When the time came, Paul went on the best trip of all and that was just the beginning of a new phase of God's plan for him and for all those others who have followed!

Questions for individual or group use may be found in the Appendix, which begins on Page 141.

2

A BRIDGE OVER TROUBLED WATERS

Spanning the Connecticut River between Cornish, New Hampshire and Windsor, Vermont is the longest covered bridge in the United States. For more than one hundred years, it has connected these two communities and states, surviving hurricanes, floods, and ice jams. However, engineers discovered structural deterioration and judging it to be unsafe, closed it to all traffic. It was decided to restore the bridge, a project that took more than two years. In the meantime, all traffic was diverted to other bridges, many miles away. It was a great day for those who found it necessary to commute to work or school when the bridge was finally opened again. Bridges can be very important!

I am thinking about another kind of "bridge," one between earlier, easier times and today's frantic "now" generation. Perhaps those of us over sixty don't realize it, but we are the only "living" bridge across that span of time and events. Did you ever stop to think that one of your goals for retirement would be to become a "bridge"?

Time and events have dictated that our generation is the most important bridge to the recent past in history. The reason for this is "acceleration." More changes have taken place in terms of monumental social and political events since World War I than in any other period of human history. What we have today are two tides going in opposite directions. One is fueled by science and technology resulting in easier living, while the other moving against it is the decline of morality. The end result is a world filled with fantastic devices and discoveries and people who don't know how to use them for the good.

Just a few short decades ago life was much more simple, and as you thumb back through the pages of earlier times, you can't help seeing that solutions were simpler, too. For example, there is a church in Cornish, New Hampshire, which, according to the "Cornish History Book" has a most unusual history. Among the events in its illustrious past was a visit by Teddy Roosevelt, the great environmentalist president. Another interesting event happened in the earlier days when the Unitarian-Universalistic movement was at its height in New England. It seems that part of the congregation was Baptist and part became Unitarian and there was a feud over who owned the church building. The case wound up in court and the judge, frustrated by the religious wrangling finally did what any good judge would have done. He decided that on a certain Sunday the congregation would gather outside the church and at a specified time, the church bell would ring. The doors would be thrown open and whichever group took over the pulpit would prevail.

The record says the Unitarians entered the church first but the Baptists overcame them as they raced down the aisle, trampled them and took over the pulpit first! That ended the confusion - the church is still Baptist and the court case cost less than ten dollars!

Since World War II it is estimated that the legislators of our country and states have passed more than fifty thousand new laws and the rate of new legislation is constantly accelerating. In addition, the courts have adapted old laws to changing times at an alarming rate. Thus, life and society is changing at an ever increasing pace. That is why it is so important that we are bridges to the past.

Can you remember a kinder, gentler time:
1. When your car and home doors could be left unlocked?
2. When you could walk safely in the city streets at night without being accosted?

3. When, if you saw a crime being committed, you would report it?
4. When society by its moral values set standards of acceptable behavior?
5. When school days began with lessons on basic health instead of lessons on AIDS, condoms, and drugs?

Some time ago, a young unidentified woman was hit by a car in Manhattan. The luxury sedan that hit her sped off into the traffic without stopping. A large crowd of onlookers stood their distance as a young man ran up to the dying woman and ripped away her pocketbook. A group of hardhat workmen finally came to prevent other cars from running over the body.

Part of the changing role of our lives, moving into retirement, is to become a bridge back to a better time. But in order to do that we must answer a question first. In our retirement will we become "crotchety" or "mellow"?

One of the strongest urges of man is possessiveness, or the desire to own. It comes right on the heels of hunger and sexual drive. Since it is a natural and God-given desire of man, taken in its proper perspective, it need not be wrong or sinful. However, possessiveness can easily turn into greed and assertiveness. This takes different forms with which we are all too familiar - political power, excessive financial greed, physical, mental, and sexual abuse. These are results of the core cause of the possessiveness syndrome which is really selfishness. Volumes have been written on this subject and the Bible gives it extensive coverage.

I would like to discuss a form of possessiveness that might be a little different, but which I am convinced affects many older people. Perhaps it affects older Christians to a somewhat greater degree. This chapter deals with our changing roles as we grow older and the implications of those changes. Even if we have no great leadership position, we will inevitably be affected by the changing of roles.

The men of Bethshemish took the Ark of the Covenant prisoner and proceeded to hold it hostage. As a result, God sent a plague upon them, something the King James Version called "emerods" (in modern day language, hemorrhoids). There is a similar plague in our time - something called "emeritus." According to the dictionary, "emeritus" can mean to "serve out one's term" or "retired as for age, with a title corresponding to that held in active service."

Now, the problem is not with "emeritus" as an honorary title such as "pastor emeritus," but with the unwillingness to hand over the authority that goes with it. There is no greater plague to a young pastor than a "pastor emeritus" who insists on continuing to have authority over a congregation that rightly belongs to the younger pastor for his own better or worse effort.

It is not only in the church that there are "emeriti." Too many of us as we grow older cannot adapt to the changing roles connected with age, and many of us have made no preparation for this inevitability. We know that our experiences have given us knowledge, and hopefully wisdom, to deal with life. Yet, after we're sixty, who wants to listen to us? How many pulpit committees are out there looking for potential pastors over age fifty-five? This evokes a response which often results in a growing determination to hang on to power and position and creates an "Osama bin Laden" type of figure!

One of the problems then, in regard to role changing is the fact that we know the answers and we want to share them, but few are willing to listen. You'll see what I mean if you listen to the talk shows on radio. Almost every older caller apologizes or in some other way indicates his or her age. He or she then conveys the thought that for that reason others might not be interested in his or her ideas. Although this is tragic, it is true. With the exception of older statesmen and politicians who seem to be in vogue, most older people have to move over and make room for the younger generation. The solution lies in the ability to instruct without control. Yet often the new leader will not listen!

The tragedy of this can be illustrated by the story in the Old Testament of Rehoboam, the son of Solomon. When he became king, the economy of Israel was in shambles. He had two groups of advisors - one young, with no previous experience, and the other older with years of service. He wanted to know whether he should raise the taxes on the people. The older group said no; the people were already overburdened with taxes. The younger group said "go ahead" and tax them. He took the advice of the younger counselors, and as a direct and immediate result there was a revolution and the nation of Israel was split forever, and irretrievably so.

I think there is a way to solve this problem and I am personally trying to apply it to my life. We can gently and happily move from the role of dynamically involved leader to a more diminished role of advisor and counselor, providing we lay the right ground work. First, we must really believe in the younger people we have gathered around us. We must entrust them with decision making, even if sometimes we think they are wrong. Secondly, we must gain their confidence that we are not about to step back in or overshadow them in the role that we have given up. We cannot be "Indian givers" in regards to the giving of responsibility.

I have come to believe that our personality goes in one of two directions when we come to the "other side of life." One I call "crotchety"! Unfortunately, many people take this path. I believe that this personality defect is directly related to our inability to adapt to the changing of roles. Crotchety, by my definition is "a pain in the neck or some other part of the body, mean, picky, always arguing." With all the other battles with growing older who needs a "crotchety" individual to make their day?

On the other hand, there is the possibility of "mellowing." This means "mature, fully developed - also made sweet or gentle by maturity." What a great goal to strive for. Maturity can take that rough, hard headed, self-centered individual and, given the right opportunity, can produce a gentle man or woman. Isn't it exciting that by its very nature, maturity coupled with God's guiding hand can make you and me better people in our older age.

Mellowing is a growth process, even as Christian growth and

the deeper and fuller life can be. It took us a long time to become the person we are and it will no doubt take us a long time to become the person we want to be. But, what a great motivation this is. I wonder how many of us, while contemplating retirement and counting our bank accounts, IRAs and mutual funds in preparation, thought about the fact that the later years of our life can be marked by a "mellowing" of our life! Such a process will make us a better, more complete happy person.

General MacArthur, our World War II hero, probably could have run for President, but chose not to. He made a famous speech at West Point in which he used that great quotation, "Old soldiers never die, they just fade away." Fading away and mellowing are not synonymous, because mellowing suggests a growing relationship with others while fading away implies a separation from others. Older Christians do not die, and they shouldn't fade away, but instead they should just "mellow." Perhaps a better way to put it would be this, "The fruit of the Spirit is love, joy, peace, longsuffering, forgiveness...." A truly mellow, truly mature Christian is a man or woman being filled with the Spirit and that is something worth striving for.

There is no need to develop anxieties about your memorial, either. In all likelihood, no matter what steps you take to insure your remembrance, you'll be forgotten in the not too distant future. Really, isn't that the way it should be? Memorials are important only because they represent acts, people, or ideals. The elders of Israel erected a monument called "Ebeneezer" to forever remind their children of God's presence and blessing upon them. It didn't work! Not long thereafter, it was Gideon, who responded to the Lord's calling, and asked, "Where are the miracles and blessings once bestowed upon Israel?" The lesson is that each new generation of God's people must know and experience for themselves the presence of God, or for that matter, any other important historical event. We can and should leave living memorials in the continuing lives of our children, family, friends, and those we have affected for Christ. Our emphasis should be more in that area than to name something after ourselves as some have done. 2 Corinthians 4:18 says, "So we fix our eyes not on what is seen, but on what is unseen. For what is seen is temporary, but what is unseen is eternal." Thus, we leave behind "living" memorials!

Another contribution we can make to the future is to teach the truth about the past. We have witnessed the Chinese propaganda machine rewriting the facts of history in the student rebellions. Many of the history writers and teachers of today in our secular colleges and schools are currently doing exactly the same thing. For example, one cannot read the early writings and statements of our country's founders without being struck by the profound part that belief in God had in their personal lives and in the events of those early days. One cannot read the great documents or speeches of our leaders without understanding that personal faith and religion played a very important role in every aspect of our country's life. Yet the liberal historians and the media would have us believe that religion was of no significance in the development of our great land.

As older citizens and as Christians, we need to make a definite commitment to make these historical facts known to every younger person we can. Colossians 4:5-6 says, "Be wise in the way you act to outsiders, make the most of every opportunity. Let your conversation be always full of grace, seasoned with salt, so that you may know how to answer everyone." Whether it be in teaching or just plain living we need to find the right mix of seasoning.

Let me propose a priority list for a pleasing personality for those on other side of life. At the very top I would place "consistency." Our partner, and our family and friends all need to count on us to be like Jesus - the same yesterday, today, and in the future. Being the same, though, does not mean that we cannot improve or change for the better. It means that we have learned how important a stable, consistent life is to ourselves and to others.

In the second place I would put "caring." When I began to seriously consider the changing of my role as President and Chairman of the Board, Pastor, and Chaplain, one of the problems that confused me was in my new, more diminished role, what ACTUAL things could I do to serve God? I found that simply to say to the Lord that I committed my life to Him for service each day sometimes left me cold and empty at day's end. I could not account for one solid act of service. All my activities had been of a general nature. Granted, they were associated with my love for God and desire to serve.

Gradually, I began to pray a different kind of prayer, attuned to my changing role. My old prayer might have been for wisdom in making important decisions, such as appropriating funds, or dealing with personnel's special requests. My new daily commitment prayer goes something like this: "Dear Lord, I commit my life to you for service today and I pray that you will bring into my path specific opportunities to serve and witness for you. Let me do today at least one special act of love toward someone in my life and let it reveal the love of Christ in me." My old prayer, contained more self-reliance and ambiguousness in my daily planning. Now my dependence is wholly on God to plan my day. A good move!

A continuing sense of humor is an absolute MUST for your retirement personality. Aside from your strong consistent faith and warm, caring attitude, nothing is more important to you and those around you than a good sense of humor. This I learned as Veterans' administration Chaplain, assigned to the cancer ward of a regional hospital. Although the atmosphere of death and dying were always present, I discovered that every patient I dealt with welcomed a smile, an encouraging word, and a good joke or comment.

Most of them had had their fill of scowling faces and forlorn looking visitors. Most of them knew the score, but wanted to make the best of every good moment. I found that a careful mix of spiritual help with a few good smiles and laughs went a long way toward responsiveness on the part of the patient. I found that if we could laugh together, then we could talk about matters of the soul. In our laughter, often the joke was on me!

On one occasion, I was called in the early morning hours to

visit a patient who had been put on the "Seriously Ill" list by the doctors. This was sort of a medical "last rites," and it was a regulation that we chaplains be called to pray with or over the patient. In this particular case, upon my arrival at the hospital, I was given the room number and name of the patient, but told that he was comatose and it would be of little use to visit him. He was a little Scotchman, named MacAllister. As I entered the room, I saw this pathetic looking figure with only his head extending above the covers. I gently bent over him and began to whisper a prayer in his ear. At that precise moment, much to my surprise, Mr. MacAllister, with a sudden motion, sat bolt upright in bed, and looking straight into my eyes said, "I don't want, any of 'that' stuff"! I guess you could call it "spiritual resuscitation." Fortunately, after I explained that I was only trying to pray for him, he consented and we did pray, and he did recover.

On another occasion, I was called to pray for a man who was going to have an operation on the following day. It was quite late in the evening when I arrived and went to "B" ward, looking for the gentleman. I was told that he was in room 212. However, when I arrived at the room, no one was there. Returning to the Nurses' station, I inquired about Mr. Franklin, who was nowhere to be seen. The Nurse said that she had seen him enter the men's restroom and would notify him that I was there. She opened the door, and shouted, "Mr Franklin there's someone here to see you." In a few moments, the door opened and out came a man wearing two hearing aids. As he came near, I said, "Mr. Franklin, I understand that you'll be having surgery tomorrow morning," whereupon he said, "What?" In a much louder voice I repeated, "I hear you'll be having surgery tomorrow morning."

At that point the message evidently got through and a thoroughly panicked patient shouted back at me, "I'm not having another operation. I'm just getting over this one"! Well, it turned out that this was not Mr. Franklin - he was still in the restroom. When the uproar was over, and I finally found Mr. Franklin, we did have prayer and I'm glad to report that he recovered nicely from his hemorrhoid operation the next day.

I feel like I inherited a good sense of humor from my parents, but it seems strange that I learned so much more while working in a hospital. One night, I came walking into the lobby with my attache case. There happened to be a single patient sitting there, probably waiting for a visitor. As I passed by, he said in a casual voice, "Evening Doc." So I stopped and asked him if he was prepared for his operation in the morning. After his initial reaction, and after I had explained that I was only the Chaplain, we had a pretty good laugh. I found that this approach opened the door to a friendship and further spiritual counseling.

I think you'll find that there are a lot of folks out there who need plenty of smiles and laughs, and these need not be as a result of off color or crude remarks. I am convinced that homespun, self-deprecating humor is often the best. A good fish story, of course, postscripted by the truth, is effective or perhaps a "Vermont" story. I do believe that if we laugh together, we can share together even the deepest most heartfelt moments.

While we're on the subject of fulfilling our role during the "challenge" years, there's another important consideration. In order to be able to serve the Lord in some specific task, we must be worthy. By that, I mean that though we might not withdraw from His service, God can remove that privilege from us. Paul thought of it in this way, "I have learned to control my body lest, after I have preached to others, I might become a castaway myself" (1 Corinthians 9:27). The analogy in his mind is of the old quill used in ancient times by the scribes. Over time they became not good enough to be used, but too good to be thrown away - a collectors item put on the shelf. I don't want to be such a relic!

I have never had a fear of losing my salvation, since there are abundant Scriptures that speak of God's enduring relationship with me as His child, one that is entirely in His hands. However, I have a very deep concern about His willingness to let me serve, and I see this as a continuing question of worthiness. I believe the Scriptures indicate that my ability to serve the Lord is directly related to the kind of life I live. Even though I may have served for thirty or forty years, or even longer, I can be decommissioned at any time. The Scripture above related "self-control" to preaching. Another applicable passage is Romans 12:1-2, where Paul pleads for the Christians to "present your bodies a living sacrifice, holy, acceptable to God, which is your reasonable service. And be not conformed to this world: but be ye transformed by the renewing of your mind that ye may prove what is that good, and acceptable, and perfect, will of God."

The kind of retirement we should seek as Christians is not to be put on the shelf like a worn out tool, but to be useful and used by the Lord within the framework of His plan for our life. This requires a constant renewing of the spirit and mind!

Questions for individual or group use may be found in the Appendix, which begins on Page 141.

······· 3 ········

IF THE SHIP LEAKS, IS IT SINKING?

The next few chapters are about anxieties after sixty that can rob us of many years of happy, healthy living. It seems like part of the maturing process should enable us to better handle the problem of anxiety. After all, by the time we're fifty-five or sixty, we probably have personally or vicariously experienced almost every possible situation that life has. The worst, most horrible scenarios are brought into our living rooms by TV on a daily basis. Yet anxiety, as it is translated into our personal lives, can produce such effects as depression, high blood pressure, strokes, and heart attacks.

In our desire for an honest self-appraisal, we must deal with our anxieties. In order to do this, we need to define them, not so much in general terms as in specifics and how they affect us individually. Of course, it is probably true that the same anxieties affect most "seniors," but not necessarily in the same order or with the same results.

Number one on my list is health, both my own and that of my family and friends. I suspect, too, that this would be number one on the "anxiety" list of most seniors. I believe the reason for this is that we are "in" our body and can't escape the sensations related to it. Nor can we escape the continual commentaries and warnings associated with our health coming from every source, including our mother, the doctor, and the TV. Some of these warnings are reliable and encourage good health practices while others seek to appeal to the ego as money making schemes. Primary among our concerns are "inevitable" health problems that arise from what I call "too much mileage."

I once attended a pre-appointment seminar conducted by a chiropractor as a prerequisite for treatment. In it, he contended that the human body is designed for 120 years of service, and given all the right conditions and care, it should live that long, in good health. Such a premise would seem to have some credence since there are many people living today well over a hundred years of age. Of course, in his opinion, chiropractic care should play a major role.

Centenarians often disagree on what enabled them to outlive the vast majority, although most agree that living a basically clean, good life was a major contributing feature. Yet there are external factors ever more evident today that affect our health, environmental factors over which we have no immediate personal control. Sometimes it seems that everything we touch, eat, or breathe contains health threatening elements.

On the other hand, there is "mileage." Like the parts of an auto, some of our body parts wear out as the years go by. Some can be repaired, some can be replaced, but some can end up beyond repair. Acceptance of the inevitability of the "wearing out" process of the body is part of the victory over health anxiety.

If in the continuing course of our life, when something goes wrong or no longer functions as it should, we move into action. First, we commit to our spiritual partner and friend the Lord Jesus Christ in prayer, then to our human partner and friends, then to our physician. The doctor then proceeds to use every available means to work with us to restore our health. When you put together a team, including the Lord, your family and friends, a competent physician, the best of medications and surgery and a fighting spirit, you've got a winning combination. Should all of this fail, our bodies are still the "temple of the Holy Spirit" and our commitment is found in Romans 14:8, "For whether we live, we live for the Lord and whether we die, we die unto the Lord: whether we live, therefore, or die, we are the Lord's."

Just because the ship is leaking, it may not be sinking, but if it is, our security is in our relationship with Christ, to whom we belong! Of course, when we know that our body is the actual temple of God's Holy Spirit, it creates or should create on our part, a personal sense of responsibility toward our health.

That brings me to the second part of our "health" discussion, which I have entitled, "two pairs of pants." It pertains to that part of our health situation that we can do something about. Many older Christians today are "food conscious." While you are not necessarily what you eat, surely what you take in as nourishment has something to do with your health. For my own part, I feel that the key word here is one of the gifts of the Spirit mentioned in Galatians 5, "temperance." I personally haven't seen any evidence that food fanaticism produces any health benefits and any possible bodily gains are usually offset by negative mental and emotional by-products. For many years, we operated a large cafeteria in connection with our ministry, and it was our experience that "vegetarians" almost without exception look unhealthy and sallow in complexion. However, not wishing to be judgmental, it may be that their particular choice of diet was for another more pressing reason. In fact, if a particular diet is needed or prescribed or even desired, then I don't classify that as "food fanaticism."

The Scripture says that all foods are gifts of God and should be received as such with thanksgiving. Romans 14:2-3 say, "One man's faith allows him to eat everything, but another man whose faith is weak eats only vegetables. Then the man who eats everything must not look down on him who does not and the man who does not eat everything must not condemn the man who does, for God has accepted him."

Diets are not to be sources of divisiveness. But let me get back to my own problem - two pairs of pants. I have found that my weight fluctuates with the seasons to the point where it has become necessary for me to have two sets of clothes. I suspect that this is not just my problem. In the later spring and all the way into the fall, my waist size fluctuates between 35-38 inches. What happens then is that my pants and even my shirt won't fit as we get in the later fall and winter months. After careful contemplation, I have come to the conclusion that part of the cause is those great holiday feasts that usher in the indoor season. A second contributing factor is surely the tendency to nibble on goodies during breaks. However, the bottom line I have decided, for me, is the change in my exercise habits. "Temperance" in weight control and ultimately health control is to find a balance between the kinds and volume of food that I eat and the exercise I engage in. It boils down to two important words "self control."

In regards to health for the Christian senior there is another significant matter, one which very few ever discuss. That is the subject of admonishing and the willingness to be admonished. Admonishing does not mean to be a spiritual "policeman" patrolling the Christian landscape, looking for likely candidates. To the contrary, admonishing must be done in the spirit of loving concern and in a setting of friendship. But there is a great need within the Christian community for seniors with adequate experience and wisdom to have the courage to admonish the many Christians of all ages who are hurting, even killing their bodies with excess fat and other self consuming habits.

It brings to mind a young man who attended a retreat at our facility several years ago. This young man weighed in excess of four hundred pounds. In effect, he was a social prisoner within his huge body. In addition, it was clear that he was hurting himself with food! While he was certainly an object of discussion by others, no one seemed willing to confront him about his obvious problem. Could it be that no one really cared or perhaps had the "guts" to approach him as a friend? As for me, the motivating climax came after a delicious spaghetti dinner. When everyone else had finished, I witnessed this young man going about the tables, collecting unfinished spaghetti and bread from the serving bowls and consuming them himself.

Later that evening, I sat down and confronted him with the fact that he was literally killing himself with food! I stressed the many good reasons he had for living, as well as emphasizing his good points, his good features, and his intelligence! I found him very receptive and appreciative that I could care and share with him as a friend.

I wish this story had a happy ending, but this young man, a member of a Christian youth group, was addicted to food and committed suicide by eating himself to death. As a postscript, however, his mother and family had remembrances sent to our ministry as a special thanks for our love for him. His mother said that his experience at the retreat was the most meaningful event in his life and she deeply appreciated my love and concern for her son.

Admonishing and being admonished is a two-way street. I can illustrate this with the experience of a middle-aged patient who came to me for counseling at the VA hospital. His story was a common one in evangelical circles. Here was a veteran, a "born again" Christian with multiple problems. He was attending a local evangelical church, but among other things, he had a smoking habit. He also had family problems, emotional and service-connected mental problems, and was seeking help. He thought it would be offered from the Lord's people. Smoking was just one of his problems. He was trying to do the impossible - share the love and fellowship of a congregation that looked negatively and even frowned on his lifestyle, especially his smoking. He once described himself in a very graphic way to me. He said that when he greeted people after church, he felt just "like a big cigarette."

I gave a great deal of thought to that. It seems to me that both the church people and the man, himself, were at fault. On one side, the people were being judgmental, spiritual "policemen," if you will. As far as this individual was concerned, their most important concern was his dirty smoking habit. On the other hand, his response was to seek justification for a devastating health problem which he confided to me was wrong and hurtful.

Once again the Scriptures have the answer in 2 Timothy 2:24: "And the Lord's servant must not quarrel, instead, he must be kind to everyone, able to teach, not resentful. Those who oppose him, he must gently instruct, in the hope that God will grant them repentance, leading to a knowledge of the truth."

While we're on the subject of health, let me share a discovery I recently made, one which I should probably keep secret. As teenagers, we had a little chorus that we sang on our trips that went like this, "Oh, you can't get to heaven on powder and paint, 'cause it'll make you look just like you ain't." That song expressed the superficial evangelical doctrine of the time - don't use cosmetics to change your appearance.

Then, one time in a chapel service at Kings College, Percy Crawford, the President and well known evangelist of the 40s and 50s, gave us a great bit of advice. It went like this: First, we should look attractive for the Lord as His ambassador. Cosmetics and grooming can be helpful as long as they are not overemphasized. In short, we should look the best we can within the "body framework" that God has given us. Even those with bodily deformities and handicaps can be attractive. Some of the most attractive people I know are not the best looking people I know.

That is how I came, after much consideration, to use "Grecian Formula." I call this experience, "How to lose weight immediately, without self-torture, diet, or exercise" - just color your hair! I had concluded that the old man in the mirror with the white hair could probably look younger, since my eyebrows were still black. At any rate, while on our extended vacation in Florida, I decided that it would be worth the effort to try it, and believe it or not, after a few days my hair began to look and feel different. Whether this was just an apparition, I don't know, but I guess the feeling was what counted. At any rate, I returned to my family and friends at the end of our holiday.

Would you believe that no one mentioned my hair for a number of weeks? I could take this as a compliment or it could mean that no one had paid any attention to me before I left. But the interesting thing is that a large number of people told me how great I looked and asked how much weight I had lost. So, if you want to painlessly lose weight, at least in your imagination, color your hair! But above all, try to be attractive for Jesus Christ and seek good health, just don't make it the god of your life.

Questions for personal or group use begin on Page 141.

······· *4* ········

Don't Throw That Club!

As we grow older, it becomes more important than ever that we choose quality friends. Of course the very best place to find such is at the church of your choice, but often the true mettle of these potential friends hasn't been put to the test. The golf course is the place to do that!

A golf course can be defined as a place of green grass, long, carefully manicured fairways and greens, beaches called sand traps and beautiful lagoons and streams - all just beckoning you to come with your lethal weapons and innocent little white balls to do battle. The place itself is a contradiction. It can put a smile on your face, reduce you to a walking blob, or send you on your way, a raving maniac. That is why it is a great place to find "quality" friends.

A "quality" friend in this instance is not necessarily any of the aforementioned. He or she is one who can "rejoice with those who rejoice, mourn with those who mourn, and weep with those who weep." But watch out for those who throw their clubs!

I was invited for an afternoon of golf with some of the administration people from the Veterans' Hospital. We were playing at a local championship course and the game was going about as usual, here and there, over and under, in and out! I was finding solace in the philosophy that I have always maintained that "hackers" have more fun! My partner was a good friend, an excellent golfer, and a stickler for the rules. In my case, a mulligan here or there didn't really matter. In fact, I didn't mind invoking the "Barnabas" rule at times (kicking your partner's ball out of an unplayable lie onto the fairway, to help his morale). No matter how well I played though, my friend always beat me. But this day it was going to be different. I was ahead! We came to the fifteenth tee and I drove long and straight down the middle. I was getting really excited about the possibility of winning for the first time when he drove his first ball out of bounds. I secretly thought, *It's all over.*

Overcome with generosity, I even went a step further and offered to go down the fairway and watch for his second drive, an offer he accepted. As I watched, his second shot hit in the fairway across from me and with a special little bounce, nestled in the branches of a thick blue spruce. I ran across the fairway as Maynard drove up in the cart. I sort of compassionately said, "Don't worry, I know right where it is," thinking to myself, *Right up in that tree, it's unplayable - that's another two stroke penalty - just enough to sew up the match.* But, as I moved into the bushes, I somehow brushed against the spruce tree and guess what? Out popped the ball, landing in the fairway with a beautiful lie. "Gee, thanks," said Maynard! I think you know what happened then! His next shot rolled up and stopped right near the flag on the green, while mine dribbled into the "beach" to the right. That opened the floodgates of disaster and with a three hole fiasco on my part, Maynard wound up winning by four strokes.

But something else happened in the meantime! I was still mumbling unintelligible sounds under my breath as we drove down the path toward the next tee where another foursome was in the process of teeing off. As we approached, Maynard touched my arm and said, "Don't get too close, this guy might throw. . . ."

He stopped in mid-sentence as the stout, red faced man, on the tee, obviously suffering from high blood pressure, wound up, spun around, and let his five iron fly! It whistled through the air and landed with the sound similar to that of a toilet plunger in a swampy area not very far from where we were parked. That sparked a flurry of unmentionable shouts and grunts, as he stalked over to the spot where the iron was buried up to the grips in the mud. *I'm glad I'm with Maynard*, I thought! As you probably know by now, this story has a lot to do with choosing the right friends.

After Maynard was transferred to Atlanta, I often thought about how much I missed my golfing buddy, even though he always beat me. I even missed his legalistic attitude. Perhaps it was because, as a friend, Maynard gave me a goal I could shoot for that seemed to be always just out of reach. At any rate, he and I had lots of laughs and even shared some sorrow on the golf course. On one particular afternoon, we had an experience together that I will always remember. As we were coming in, toward the clubhouse, from the eighteenth green, one of the pros came out and told Maynard that he had an important phone call. I'll never forget the look on his face as he came out of the pro shop toward me - there were tears in his eyes. "I just found out that Ellen has breast cancer," he said. "I don't know what to do!" It was an opportunity for me to put my arm around him and, together, we lifted up his wife in a short prayer. I'm glad to say that Ellen completely recovered after surgery.

Yes, playing golf will have its laughs and, sometimes, even tears, but it can be one of the many good ways of finding friends. Only stay away from those who throw their clubs! And, oh yes, there did come a day when I beat my old pal by one stroke - miracles do happen!

I debated for some time with myself about which anxiety should come second on my list for seniors. Since I was writing at a time when the lack of money was of great concern to me, I was tempted to put "finances" in second place. However, as I considered life in these challenging years, I realized that relationships were of even more importance to me and thus potentially a greater source of anxiety.

As we grow older, there seems to be what we might call the "law of diminishing returns" in our social life. The harsh reality of this is that over a period of time it results in less close friends, less social activities, and ultimately in a "closed" life. One can see the tragic result in nursing homes where row after row of elderly people sit rocking their life away. While some of these are mentally or physically incapacitated, many others could still be leading a happy, fulfilled life. What is worse, once started, this unfortunate turn of events gains momentum.

As older Christians, we must fight the tendency to withdraw. More teaching in the New Testament is about relationships than about any other subject - and for good reason. We must seek to continue to establish new, mutually inspiring relationships as the years pass. Otherwise, the inroads of time, illness, geographic change, and role change will diminish our relationships with others. The church, the Body of Christ, is commanded to play a major role in the relationship experience of believers. To do this, however, there needs to be a responsive attitude on our part. We cannot afford to become introverted. We must make the effort to seek out friends with whom we can have pleasure and good conversation. This is important, not only to you but also to God. Malachi 3:16-17 says, "Then those who feared the Lord talked with each other and the Lord listened and heard. A scroll of remembrance was written in His presence concerning those who feared and honored His name. 'They will be mine', says the Lord Almighty, 'in the day when I make up my treasured possession.'"

A true friendship is one that has a "basis." For the Christian, it is founded in an understanding of the love of Christ and the teachings of the Bible. The products of a true Christian friendship ought to be encouragement, joy, and shared blessing. Honesty and loyalty are always present. There can be unhappy moments, but these will be overshadowed by warmness and sharing, and if necessary, forgiveness.

May I suggest several ways that we can determine whether a relationship is worth pursuing? First, a good relationship should not produce anxiety. A misspoken word, a late arrival, a difference of opinion - these should not produce apprehension and anxiety. Such trivialities should not interrupt a real relationship. They do need to be handled and the Scriptures tell us how, but they will never bring down a relationship worth building. A soft answer not only turns away wrath, but also is valuable in solving all kinds of friendship problems.

I would like to tell you about my "flock" idea. I feel that in a sense, we Christians are "undershepherds" of a small "flock" that the Lord has put in our lives. At the same time, we are all members of that same flock. This idea has two dimensions - the one is that we are to care for that special flock and the other is that the "flock" is to care for us, a mutual relationship. The flock that I am to care for in a special way consists of my family and friends who are in the "inner circle" of my life. On the spiritual level, these are the ones whom I lift up in particular, specific prayer, ones who I try to encourage in every spiritual way that I can. This produces a sense of security in my most intimate relationships and reduces any anxieties that I might have. At the same time, I am part of the flock, and they will care for me! Jesus said, "I am the Good Shepherd and I give my life for the sheep." The human flock of which I am a part is the embodiment of Jesus' relationship with His people on the deepest, most meaningful level of life. The interrelationships springing from our common love for Christ and the beauty of life that proceeds from Him are the very best available to you and me.

On the other hand, it is possible as life proceeds to become a hermit or recluse, but this is not what God wants for any of us. Come out of that house, overcome that fear, defeat that timidity - let the Lord show you the beauty and thrill of sharing His love with others. Let your circle of friends increase rather than decrease as you grow older.

Relationships usually grow out of common interests and while the church provides the basic meeting ground, there are many other venues, too. I'll use just two illustrations from our own experience. In this case, one concerns the men and the other concerns the women. Now, golf is definitely a psychological pursuit. It is known to produce feelings of anger, depression, and downright disgust. More jokes have been told about golf than any other sport. I think golf is a great testing ground for relationships, not because of its competitiveness but because of the abundance of feelings it produces. Without the element of humor, golf becomes a dangerous game for friends!

Golf can also be very humorous. Imagine this scenario -

you're playing with three of your very competitive golfing buddies. The match is even coming into the last two holes and you are about to tee off on the seventeenth. You're becoming more serious and determined, even intense. You tee up, you're over the ball, and you're in the back swing. At that precise moment, a large workhorse that had been leaning over the fence in the adjacent field, watching you, lifts his head in the air and whinnies in a loud, long, and high pitched tone. The club comes down with a mighty swing and the ball proceeds to trickle down the front of the tee and into the bushes in front of the horse. Now, what would a really good friend do? My friends roared with laughter, but they didn't offer me a "mulligan"!

For the ladies there is the "yard sale circuit." I define a yard sale as a "circle of junk orbiting a community or neighborhood within a given radius and eventually returning to its source." However, yard sales provide a great opportunity for ladies to explore, always looking for that special treasure and sometimes, if rarely, finding it. Yard sales, like golf, can have their moments of triumph and their moments of devastation. To discover a special treasure overlooked by the hordes of invaders and to decide to spend fifty cents only to have a greedy hand reach out and grab the item, can be devastating. On the other hand, my good wife usually comes home with some exciting bargain, which, unknown to the seller, was of great value, and her friend does the same. At the next neighborhood yard sale, we will try to make a small profit on our "investments" as we return the items to "orbit."

The point of all this is that, if we want relationships that are meaningful, we must do things together. We must cultivate "friendships." Whether they are fun activities or deep experiences, the laughs and the conversations will contribute to a relationship that lasts.

Questions for individual or group use may be found in the Appendix, which begins on Page 141.

5

BANK ACCOUNTS, IOUs, AND BOUNCING CHECKS

Number three on my list of anxieties and perhaps the most dramatic of all is the subject of finance. Probably more books have been written, advice given, and time spent on the subject of money than on any other subject. It was not too long ago that many Christians felt that providing for security during retirement constituted a lack of faith.

Mission boards had no retirement plan and pastors and other Christian workers rejected "social security." It was thought that this was an important spiritual decision, a demonstration of faith. As a consequence, there are many older Christian workers today living at or below the poverty level in their retirement years. There are obviously many other senior Christians who neglected to, or were unable to, make provision for their later years, financially, and the results are devastating to some. Not only can they not maintain the lifestyle that they had for many years, but they cannot afford necessary medical and dental treatment. Their retirement has become a struggle for survival, and the circumstances produce a prolonged and growing anxiety, an element undeserved and surely not needed in the process of growing old. Can anything be done?

It seems to me that we must again go back to the beginning, to the bottom line, which is: Do we truly believe God? There are two particular ideas that we need to review often. One is "provision" and the other is "peace." As for the first, Jesus had much to say about God, the Father, caring for us and as a result of His caring, providing. Take another look at Matthew 6:25-34: "Therefore I tell you, do not worry about your life, what you will eat or drink; or about your body, what you will wear. Is not life more important than food, and the body more important than clothes? Look at the birds of the air; they do not sow or reap or store away in barns, and yet your heavenly Father feeds them. Are you not much more valuable than they? Who of you by worrying can add a single hour to his life? And why do you worry about clothes? See how the lilies of the field grow. They do not labor or spin. Yet I tell you that not even Solomon in all his splendor was dressed like one of these. If that is how God clothes the grass of the field, which is here today and tomorrow is thrown into the fire, will he not much more clothe you, O you of little faith? So do not worry, saying, 'What shall we eat?' or 'What shall we drink?' or 'What shall we wear?' For the pagans run after all these things, and your heavenly Father knows that you need them. But seek first his kingdom and his righteousness, and all these things will be given to you as well. Therefore do not worry about tomorrow, for tomorrow will worry about itself. Each day has enough trouble of its own" (NIV).

In this short passage, Jesus refers to worrying no less than five times. He is certainly talking about everyday life and in His time He is instructing people who had no retirement program, no bank accounts, and no government "safety net" or "catastrophic insurance."

A passage like this does, however, raise some gritty questions. Given the absence of resources in Jesus' time, was He teaching them to have no concern about their material well-being or to make no provision for the future? I don't think so.

His lesson here, if I read it correctly, is about God's "provision" and our "peace." The fact is the God DOES HAVE a "safety net" of security for His people. It is based upon the fact that He knows our needs and that as a loving and caring heavenly Father He provides for them. But I believe that there are some facts that we need to get straight. While Jesus promises here that our "needs" will be met, He did not promise "luxury living." In most of what we call the "free world" or "West" today, we have gotten so used to all the frills of affluence that we don't sometimes think of life in the same dimension as others who are less fortunate. And we have come to believe that "providing" means sumptuous living. It is a real fact that most of us Christian seniors have a lot of "fat" in our lives. Our cars could be a little smaller, our visits to the restaurants a little less often, our homes a little more modest.

God has so abundantly blessed us that we are at the very borders of "fantasy land." Should we be faced with a difficult depression, most of us would not really recognize "provision," even when it was there. It reminds us of the Israelites with the manna and quail - God's daily provision in the desert. It became so commonplace that not only did they get sick of it, they began to forget God Himself. I see that as a danger to us.

Some of us on "the other side of life" must learn to live at or below the poverty level, others with moderate means, and some with affluence. Each of these financial strata carry with them spiritual responsibility. At the high end, the problem is faith and at the low end it is also faith, both in a sense the same but very different for each other. Paul had discovered how to confront the challenge of both situations. He wrote in Philippians 4:11-13: "Not that I speak from want, for I have learned to be content in whatever circumstances I am. I know how to get along with humble means, and I also know how to live in prosperity; in any and every circumstance I have learned the secret of being filled and going hungry, both of having abundance and suffering need. I can do all things through Him who strengthens me."

Affluence brings with it the responsibility of "wealth sharing." In our plans and provision for retirement, if God has seen fit to bless us with abundant material wealth, we should and must consider the less fortunate and the needs of God's work. Again and again, in Scripture, we are taught this lesson. It is not enough to take our tithes and offerings into the storehouse of the church and fulfill an obligation. The "giving" must be more personal than a check. It should flow from a profound sense of gratitude and selflessness. There needs to be a little "hurt" in giving, especially on the part of the wealthy.

Poverty also brings responsibility, because the inevitable temptation is to blame someone or something for the circumstance. Poverty produces the responsibility to seek out resources and help. There is a "work ethic" taught in Scripture, and while it is not physically and sometimes mentally possible for all seniors to work, the implication is that we must make an effort toward self- help, while depending on the Lord to provide.

It is hard for us in our setting to comprehend what it must be like to live in the African desert or some other bleak situation where there are no options. Christians have had to do this, and are doing it today. In our case, there are many options, beginning with government assistance, which in most cases we have earned over the years with our hard work and taxes. There are social agencies specifically targeted toward special needs. But above all, I still put the Body of Christ, the church, because God, in His Word made the church the instrument of caring for His people. For this reason, it is of utmost importance that the Christian, moving toward later life, keep the church as a focal point of his or her life. When help is needed, it will be there, provided it is a "Christ-centered church" and provided we give the church an opportunity to help.

Perhaps we can best understand what this whole discussion of anxiety is about by refreshing our memory concerning the "Spirit-motivated life." We have heard so much in contemporary evangelical circles about the "Spirit-filled" life, and for good reason. The Scripture commanded, "Do not be drunk with wine, but be filled with the Holy Spirit." Yet, I would like to suggest that the idea of being filled is only one aspect of the teaching about the Spirit at work in our lives. It is possible, as I see it, for the "Spirit-oriented life" to become superficial and, as a result, passive and benign, and ego-centric instead of reaching out to help others. Consider the fruits of the Spirit listed in Galatians 5:22-23: "But the fruit of the Spirit is love, joy, peace, patience, kindness, goodness, faithfulness, gentleness, and self-control. Against such things there is no law" (NIV).

There is an intrinsic self value in each of these fruits, but they only reproduce in their relationship to others. In other words, there is a difference in "living in the Spirit" and "walking in the Spirit" as it says in Galatians 5:25. Living in the Spirit relates to His effect upon and in us, while walking in the Spirit relates to His effect upon others THROUGH us.

That brings me to the other word in our thoughts on anxiety concerning finances, that word being "peace," one of the fruits of the Spirit. For purposes of this discussion, I would like to use the word "activated" in regard to the fruits of the Spirit as they apply to our consideration of anxiety. Let's suppose we are undergoing a real trial financially, which may or may not be of our own doing. Bills are overdue, our financial plans haven't worked out as we intended - we're in a tough situation. We may even be looking at the possibility of bankruptcy. Being retired, we go back to the drawing board and look at our options, but they seem to be bleak. We don't have all of the options possible during our younger career. This is precisely when we need "activated peace," which is derived from the fact that God is involved with us as our partner. It is then that Romans 8:26, 28 can be applied: "In the same way, the Spirit helps us in our weakness. We do not know what we ought to pray for, but the Spirit himself intercedes for us with groans that words cannot express. . . . And we know that in all things God works for the good of those who love Him, who have been called according to His purpose" (NIV).

Yes, the answers to our financial anxieties lies in the appropriation of a truth that most Christian seniors already know, the combination of the provision of a loving God with the peace of a Spirit-activated life.

Before moving on to another "anxiety," I would like to share a view that I have gained, both from a careful study of the Scriptures and a wealth of experience. Concerning the filling of the Spirit. I have come to believe that the best test of whether, and to what degree, I am "Spirit-filled" is in the intensity with which I live the "Spirit fruit" activated life in my relationship with others. This is far more important than the claims I make about my being "Spirit filled"!

Questions for individual or group use may be found in the Appendix, which begins on Page 141.

6

BELLS, BUZZERS, AND WHISTLES

This brings us to a rather obscure anxiety of the other side of life, and it has to do with "patience," another fruit of the Spirit. Patience is one of the greatest tests of self-control and a very difficult one to master. Because "time" is related to patience, it is one of the contributing factors to what we'll call "time sequence anxiety."

In manufacturing, "time" is a major factor in production, and that is a lesson taught from the earliest days of our schooling. Have we forgotten how bells and buzzers controlled our lives in the school and workplace? I was known as "Biebel at the bell" in high school because I knew just how to make it to that first period and slip into my seat just as the late bell was ringing. I can't count the number of slightly sprained ankles I had from running and stumbling up those stairs.

Bells and buzzers controlled everything in our childhood, including classes, recess, and last and most important, the moment everyone was waiting for, dismissal. The same held true for the workplace - there were bells, buzzers, and the added element of whistles. Checking in, in the morning, there was a little bell that rang when you put your card into the time clock, then a whistle blew when it was time to start work, then a buzzer rang for the coffee break, and so it was that we learned that life was a sequence of important time periods. This is not easily forgotten when we retire. Time sequence anxiety produces everything from restlessness to sleep disorders. Not only is it unhealthy for ourselves, but it is a continual nuisance to others and mostly to those closest to us. Its offspring is the inability to relax and be satisfied. Our eyes are always on the clock, we are ever on the move, and we must be at a certain place at a certain time. A favorite bumper sticker in Florida says, "life is a beach." Unfortunately to some seniors a more appropriate sticker would say "life is a time clock." Part of "maturity" is learning to overcome handicapping habits of our life, and in the case of "time sequence anxiety," perhaps the best teaching tool is experiential.

Take the case of the missing 757 for example. There are many free training schools for "patience" with absolutely no tuition charges. There's the doctors' and dentists' offices where we arrive anxiously on time only to wait with a multitude of other patients who have obviously been scheduled at the same time. While we're waiting there's that little tot whose crying voice indicates he or she will someday be an opera star, and whose nose is constantly running. Then, there are the freeways and shopping malls where we learn to control our feet and mouth.

But for my wife and I, there is the Atlanta Airport! It has been said that on our way to heaven, we'll have to change planes in Atlanta. However, my description of that place would be more like purgatory, if there were such a place, because purgatory is a place where only prayer can get you out! Let me tell you about my greatest lesson in patience.

The story begins in Melbourne, Florida. We were there at the excellent airport awaiting a flight that would terminate in Boston, with a stopover and change of planes in Atlanta. Now on this particular afternoon, the weather was bright and sunny and at the scheduled time we arrived at Gate 3, where we could look out a large window and see our plane parked just a few feet from the waiting room door. We were primed for a great flight, but the 727 had a flat tire - something I had never heard of before!

Although the Melbourne airport handles many big jets, and has excellent, modern accommodations, it was obviously not prepared to handle a flat tire. In full view of all the passengers, a slapstick comedy began to unfold during which the mechanics tried everything they could think of to change that tire. First, they brought out a small jack and proceeded to try to lift that 727. After pumping furiously, it became obvious to the mechanics that that particular jack wouldn't work. Some time later, a pickup truck arrived with a larger jack, and under the watchful eyes of the entire flight crew, the plane finally rose far enough for the wheel to be changed. Then, it was found that no one had the proper wrench to remove the lug nuts from the wheel.

At that point a small boy was playing with some plastic tools on the floor of the waiting room and someone said in a loud voice, "Sonny, why don't you go give the man the right tool," eliciting a titter of laughter from the waiting crowd. After an hour's wait, we were finally in the air on our way to Atlanta, wondering if that wheel would stay on when we landed. Of course, we were all fully aware of the fact that there was no way that we would be making our connecting flights. This was my first semester of "patience," but it was only the beginning.

Our flight to Atlanta was smooth and as we neared touchdown at Hartsfield Airport, the flight attendant announced that there would be an agent waiting as we disembarked to direct us to our connecting flight to Boston and other points. As we left the plane and headed up the ramp, little did I know that I was in reality entering a marathon race. Having been through this before, we realized that we needed to hurry, since traveling by air often becomes a survival of the fastest.

The waiting attendant tells us that our plane will be at Concourse B, Gate 19. So, bidding my wife temporarily goodbye, I dash out ahead of the throng. Down the escalator, onto the moving sidewalk, listening to the droning sound of the computer generated voice instructions, up the stairway, and zig-zag through the moving crowd.

Finally, out of breath, I am at the desk of Gate 19. Looking skeptically at me, the attendant said, "Sir, I don't know anything about this. This plane is already fully booked." By this time a whole line of people are behind me, all wanting to get on that plane.

"Sir, the best I can do is put you on standby," she says, "if you'll just give me your tickets." Well, at least I'm first in line so

I relax and sit down with my wife, who has since arrived on the scene. Why do we have a sense of impending doom?

Some forty-five minutes later, the attendant comes on the loud speaker with the news, "I'm sorry folks, but we are having mechanical difficulties and this flight has been cancelled. If you will go down to Gate 9, there will be another flight to Boston."

I'm already on the run, zigging and zagging through the crowd. Now, if you are familiar with the great airports know that it is no small feat to go from one end of the concourse to the other, even under normal circumstances. By this time, for those wanting to get on that Boston plane, the effort has become the "Boston Marathon." Unfortunately, even those who have never had the experience before are getting the idea that speed is of the essence. There is a whole phalanx of runners heading for Gate 9.

Even though I am pressing sixty years old, with my head start and good physical condition, I arrive at the next gate among the first. There we are told by the attendant to take our seats and the plane will be departing on or near schedule. It is somewhat comforting to notice that the captain and the rest of the crew are waiting with us in the same area. So begins the second semester.

At the scheduled time for departure, the girl at the desk comes back on the intercom with another message. When she begins "folks," all of our anxieties come back with a flood. "Folks," she says, "your plane is having some minor mechanical problems and right now it is in that big hanger across the runway being serviced. Please be patient and we'll have you on your way in a short time."

I take some comfort in the fact that the flight crew seem to be taking things in stride and are laughing and talking. Time slips by and the collective patience of the crowd is growing thin, but I am determined that I will win this battle with my anxiety, although this is becoming more difficult with the passing of each fifteen minutes, and still there is no plane to be seen.

I notice that the flight crew is beginning to disappear and only the captain is left, calmly reading the *New York Times* financial section. Periodically, the attendant comes on the intercom with the diminishing assurance that we'll soon be in the air. I wonder if she and we are using the same definition of "soon."

Then I have a brainstorm. The captain must know what's going on, so I ease up to him and come up with a very original question, "Captain, are we ever going to get to Boston?"

Now pilots have a certain voice tone that somehow can comfort the most troubled heart. He responds in that calm, strong voice, with words that I will always remember. "Well, I wish I could tell you. My crew and I brought your plane, a 757, into this gate about two hours ago and we stepped out to get a bite to eat. When we returned, the plane was gone. I have no idea where it went." Welcome to the third semester!

A short time later we enter the final exam. The attendant comes on and with a quivering voice says, "Folks" - that dreaded word! I am already poised for the next race, but I notice that all the others are, too. I am beginning to feel a sense of camaraderie with these people, but my sense of determination is at an all-time peak. When the new gate number is announced, it is like the starter's gun going off. The throng is off for Gate 21 where, we've been assured, there will be another plane waiting.

Now, I'm pretty fast for sixty years old and I'm right up there with the leaders, two young men. In fact, I'm in third position, right behind a red haired fellow. I can almost fantasize that we're in "Chariots of Fire," except we aren't running in slow motion. I can imagine the crowd cheering. Glancing back, I can see the whole herd of people coming ever closer. But we make it before them - finally, Gate 21, and I'm still third in line. Thank you, Lord!

I'm at the desk, almost expecting the attendant to say, "Folks," but instead she says, "Sir, may I have your tickets." The tickets! But, I don't have my tickets - they're back at Gate 9. Thank God for computers - our names must be on the computer! They are and she says with just a hint of compassion, "Sir, you and your wife will be some of the first on standby, but I can't give you your boarding pass until we're sure there'll be room."

Now I have a breather to go back and get my wife, who also

is still at Gate 9. When I arrive after a brisk walk, she and the attendant are the only two left. I go up to the attendant to regain my tickets and tell her that we just have to get on that next plane. My voice betrays something between suffering and whining. It must have touched a sympathetic heartstring, because she leans over and whispers, "Sir, if you don't tell anyone, I'll issue you your boarding passes and when you get back to Gate 21 and the announcement is made, just get on the plane."

Can it be that simple? Triumphantly, I'm on the last lap, complete with my wife, my tickets, and even a measure of patience. When our row number is called, we look neither to the left or right but move quickly and efficiently onto the plane and into our seats. We arrive in Boston some six hours late and drive into our driveway as dawn is just beginning to show in the East over the New Hampshire hills. What a glorious sunrise it is. We fall into bed knowing that we have passed our exam and received our bachelor of patience degree. Our only hope is that we don't have to go to graduate school on our next flight!

Did you ever stop to think that the process of maturation is a "time sequence." My definition of maturation is "that natural process by which we are prepared for each new phase of life." Patience is part of that process, and one of the great modern tragedies is the fact that there is no "childhood" any more. Society has opted to eliminate childhood. We are teaching first and second graders about AIDS, sex, and every other adult subject. And we are subjecting them to the worst, most degrading horror and filth in the movies and TV. Their God given "time clock" is not ready for these things yet, and they are pushed and forced into a phase of life meant for later or not meant for life at all! The same can be said about adolescents and teenagers. But there will be no return, so we must share our values and the joy of Christian living with younger people whenever the opportunity exists.

Once when I was Chaplain at the Vermont State Prison, a maximum security facility, the Warden asked me casually, one day, if I would be willing to teach a course to the inmates. Of course, I just as casually said, "Sure, what is the subject? The warden replied, "Marital felicity" whereupon I said "Oh, okay," wondering to myself, *What is felicity?* Later that evening I went to Webster and found that "felicity" can be defined as "the state of being happy, bliss." So, I found myself teaching a group of convicts, including everything from rapists to murderers, a course on happiness and bliss in marriage. One thing I'll say is that it was an extremely interesting experience and one I'll never forget.

For my material, I sought out an old course from my Gordon College days, one led by Dr. Gedney, for the purpose of counseling and instructing the married students. The main premise of the course was the subject of maturing and its relationship to the stages of life: infancy, childhood, adolescence, young adulthood, adulthood, the middle years, and the golden years. The premise was that each of these phases had a relationship to marriage. We talked about the "love is blind" stage of courtship, and the honeymoon time when nothing really mattered except "love," and differences could be overlooked. It was Dr. Gedney's theory that in marriage you go directly from the "love is blind" phase to the "reform school" phase. The reform school phase in this case was not to make the partner better, as the word might imply, but to make the person fit into your mold and lifestyle. It was at this point that many immature, totally unprepared young people couldn't handle the mental trauma and the relationship then broke down.

I was surprised when we had completed the study that a number of the men told me how they wished that they had known about these things earlier so that things might have been different. Some seniors have, in their marriage relationship, never left the reform school stage. Doesn't it seem to you that a man and a woman who have been married for thirty or forty years should be past the stage of jousting over every conceivable issue? Was Aunt Tillie married in 1928 or 1929? Did Uncle Joe fall in the river or was it the bathtub? Some of the silliest conversations ever recorded have been between Mr. and Mrs. Senior citizen.

Then too, there's the battleground of the "clothes closet." You'd think that by the time I was sixty years old, I should have known what tie or suit to wear, even though it had taken me at least fifty years to learn that stripes don't go with plaids.

I'm not kidding when I say that too many husbands and wives act more like custodians in a reform school than loving and caring partners. Do these things really matter?

This brings me back to the "time sequence anxiety" and its application to seniors. First, time to the Christian senior should be a question of priority. If we have learned any lessons in patience and acceptance of life, as it truthfully is, we have learned that we have plenty of time, and if we don't, so be it! We can be surrounded by troubles, even enemies. We can be alone, seemingly forsaken, by everyone, but we need never give in to time or to the idea of sequence which, taken together, mean inevitability. Listen to the Psalmist: "I am forgotten as a dead man, out of mind; I am like a broken vessel. For I have heard the slander of many, terror is on every side; while they took counsel together against me, they schemed to take away my life. But as for me, I trust in You, O LORD, I say, 'You are my God.' My times are in Your hand. . ." (Ps. 31:12-15).

When David used the plural word "times" to refer to the events of his life, I'm quite sure he had in mind both the main events including the exciting and dangerous experiences as well as the usual mundane experiences of everyday life. The Christian senior who has made the commitment of his or her life to Christ, will be "graced" with the gift of godly patience. All of the times and the sequences by which they unfold become a cause for praise and produce victory over anxiety.

Questions for individual or group use may be found in the Appendix, which begins on Page 141.

7

DOING BUSINESS IN GREAT WATERS - DEALING WITH CURRENT EVENTS

One of my favorite pastimes is fishing, and my favorite spot to fish is the "Sebastian Inlet," located on the East Coast of Florida. It is a dangerous spot, and there are large signs warning boaters to be extremely careful. When the tide is running out and the wind is from the East there is a tremendous turbulence. Many boats, large and small, have been swamped in the maelstrom of currents and surf. However, it is the swirling, churning water that makes the inlet one of the best fishing spots anywhere.

The rapid currents and abundant baitfish making their way into and out of the Indian River attract many species of fish, including those as large as sharks, manta rays, porpoises, and a whole array of smaller game fish. All this means that Sebastian Inlet is a mecca for every conceivable kind of boat from fourteen-foot skiffs to fifty-foot yachts.

On this particular day, my friend Charlie and I are perusing the scene in our eighteen-foot "Riviera." The pelicans are perched in their usual places in the palms that overhang the shores. They are watching for the slightest commotion on the surface, whereupon they will soar quickly to the spot and dive unceremoniously, beak first, into the school of fish hoping for a good meal. Various boats are anchored or cruising up and down the inlet seeking the best and most productive spot. They are graced with the usual bevy of girls and dogs and many of them feature an array of rods and gear that makes them resemble a miniature military installation. For Charlie and me, the order of the day is trolling.

We notice two obviously passionate fishermen in a small boat trolling by a particular marker buoy. It seems to us that just as they pass that buoy each time, they have a strike and after a prolonged fight, they boat a good-sized fish. Then there is the weather-beaten fisherman in the rickety old skiff. It obviously hasn't been painted in years and is covered with a generous combination of dirt, seaweed, and barnacles. It seems to us that this man never moves from his special spot, and yet, he keeps bringing in fish. What is the matter with us? So far we have been skunked!

By this time, we've lost three brand new lures, hung up on the rocky bottom, along with a good measure of our patience. Our lines have been tangled, one fishing hat blown overboard and lost - a typical fiasco for Charlie and me!

What brings us back another time? It is that great feeling of excitement when that big fish finally hits. With a ferocious blast, the pole bends, the line begins to feed out with a zing and it suddenly becomes a battle between man and fish and the issue is by no means settled.

Your monster is still taking out line, diving and leaping, and he is far out behind the boat. The strong current is adding to the fight. Other boats are weaving in and out threatening to foul our line and cut it. We're struggling with the motor, the rudder, the net, and each other. On this day we land a ten pound fighting "blue," but it will not make up for all the others lost in the heat and confusion of battle.

Life at the Sebastian Inlet strongly resembles our experiences as we come to "the other side of life." The characters of the Inlet are just like us. There are those restless fishermen flitting from spot to spot, ever hoping for a better catch. There is the ancient mariner staying in that one special spot. And there are people on those sleek, white yachts nearly swamping themselves on the deck with their lotion and drinks, who couldn't care less. Just like the world!

When we're talking about "doing business in great waters" we are really thinking about coping with the world around us. We're talking about currents, dangers, fish, people, equipment, knowledge, and excitement. We're out there in our little boat. Will we bring in anything, will we come in empty, or will we come in at all? We are there because that is where the "fish" are! We are there because Jesus sent us!

Coping with the world around us involves not only what happens "out there" but also what happens when the world comes to us. When we are home, we ought to be able to feel safe and secure and at rest.

Perhaps the greatest threat to that serenity is the "tube," at least that was what it used to be called when it had a tube. Through this medium, the world comes to us. Even when it was just black and white, which I can recall, the intrusion of a world presented by biased networks was sometimes a source of anxiety for me, though there was a certain element of unreality that went with seeing it all in black and white, and sometimes with lots of "snow" in the picture. Now that we have huge flat screen high definition TVs that receive their signals digitally from a satellite or cable source, the world arrives day by day in what can sometimes seem like real time three dimensional images.

This is all well and good when the images are entertaining, as with sports or wholesome movies, game shows or educational programs, or informational, such as unbiased news or special reports. But TV can be the source of anxiety when it is used for detrimental or even evil purposes, such as pornography and other filth that anyone, including young children, can welcome into the home by simply punching in the right channel number on the remote control. For those of us who treasure the morals and values of our youth, which are undermined more often than not by today's TV programming, one of our greatest anxieties is that everything we hold dear is in danger of being swept away.

My youth was very ordinary. I was born and brought up in the city of Bridgeport, Connecticut. I attended a high school that was at least partially integrated in those earlier days. Color, ethnic background, and religion were all but invisible, even though our school was a "melting pot" in 1941.

I was thirteen years old when World War II broke out and we were taught and fervently believed that our country's cause was right and that our mission was to make the world free - a better place to live. Most of our people were proud to be Americans, proud of our democratic institutions, our government, and our moral and spiritual values.

I became first a Christian and then a dedicated Christian, feeling that we needed to reach out in a demonstration of love to a world torn by war. I associated the history and future of our country, its great work ethic, and home and family traditions with what I regarded as my mission. To me there was nothing more important than the great lessons I had received from my family, my school, and the church. That is where I came from and that is what produced the man I am today.

But, there were many things that I was not aware of, daily coming into my home by way of television. Three particular words cause me a great deal of distress. One is "acceleration," another is "revisionism," and the third is "momentum." Sometimes I wonder if perhaps the great teachers I had and the history books I read were right about the past, but non-prophetic about the future. So much has changed!

Change is inevitable and is not in itself bad, but when change becomes "revisionism" it causes me great concern about the future for my children, grandchildren, and great-grandchildren. "Revisionism" to me is a kind of political or editorial rationalization of past events in order to justify present and future changes or ideals. When it goes beyond rationalization to downright bold and aggressive lying, then we know that we are in a battle for the life of our democracy. The way this affects me is in my concern for the coming generations.

Revisionism permeates every area of our lives today and the

process is gaining momentum and accelerating. And you and I as seniors have lived and are continuing to live through the greatest "acceleration" of history the world has ever seen.

Let me give you what I believe are the greatest examples of revisionism. One is exemplified by the Supreme Court in many of it decisions. Historically, it is completely incredulous to believe that the designers of our constitution and Bill of Rights conceived of or would condone some of the ludicrous issues of our time, supposedly covered by "freedom of speech." Although many of these original men were Christians, we admit that they were affected by the same temptations and some engaged in the same sins as we see today among our political leaders. Yet, in all their oratory, writings, and practices they always associated "freedom" with "responsibility."

Although they sought to protect individual rights, they saw a commitment and duty of the individual to contribute to the benefit of society. If they were here today, they would not condone, under the "free speech" amendment, such irresponsible and society damaging profiteering as pornography. And if they were here today, in all probability they would be marching with the "right to lifers," because in their time, children were thought of and valued as God-given gifts and were precious in the sight of their parents.

Revisionism is this: The very institutions which many of us saw as the bulwarks of freedom and role models for moral and spiritual values are today suspect to many ordinary citizens. The Congress, other government agencies, and particularly the Supreme Court are losing credibility with many, if not the majority, of the people. The threat of national "self-destruction" comes from the rapidly deteriorating confidence in government at precisely the time when we need to feel secure in our social affairs and feelings. Segments of the government are becoming part of the problem, part of the threat, instead of contributors to the solution.

Today, in our land, we have at least three and possibly four "power bases." I call them the "Untouchables" - that is to say, entities that the ordinary citizen cannot touch in any way with his feelings, beliefs, or ideas, even though they profoundly affect his personal life. These three entities, which have reached the zenith of power, are: the Supreme Court, the crime and drug cartel, and the entertainment industry (more specifically, Hollywood and Television). As strange as it may seem, I see these groups as interrelated, a coalition, which is especially dangerous, because in the perception of the ordinary citizen, the forces of good and evil here seem to merge. Yes, gradually but with increasing acceleration, the power of the people is becoming the power of the privileged few. The "few," in this case are not the "liberals" or "conservatives," the Whites or the Blacks.

The Supreme Court has become a supermarket for making new laws. On a regular basis the newspapers carry a list of decisions rendered by the court, covering every aspect of life from the cradle to the grave. Thoughtful people must now look with daily trepidation at the decisions to see how they will affect their personal lives. More often than not, these decisions result in less, rather than more, freedom for the majority of the people. What is worse, many of the decisions handed down have little or no relationship to the original laws or amendments as envisioned by those who drafted them. Thus, they become new laws within themselves and many of them are diametrically opposed to the will of the majority of the citizens. This is done by a small cloistered group of men and women appointed for life, whose personal political and philosophical whims are the basic contributing factor to the decisions. There is no recourse to the people.

I wish there were something humorous to say about this particular anxiety, but I fear that it is so deep and far reaching that it is different, in that it has no humorous side. I feel safe in agreeing with the polls that show that most older Americans find this to be of very deep concern to them.

Yet we must not abdicate our responsibility to be "salt and light," even in the face of such dark developments. Jesus described our proper role: "You are the salt of the earth, but if the salt loses its saltiness, how can it be made salty again? It is no longer good for anything, except to be thrown out and trampled by men. You are the light of the world. A city on a hill cannot be hidden. Neither do people light a lamp and put it under a bowl. Instead, they put it on its stand, and it gives light to everyone in the house. In the same way, let your light shine before men, that they may see your good deeds and praise your Father in heaven."

Many believers confine their fulfillment of this command of Christ to trying to be salt and light to political conservatives and other believers, but I think that Jesus had a broader meaning in mind. We are to be salt and light to the broad spectrum of people who make up our world. We are truly doing business in "great waters." Yes, we are to seek out and reach those who are liberal activists and even radicals, just as Jesus did. In order to do so, we must be intelligent, broad in knowledge, and appealing in our manner. In short, we must have the "stuff" to reach out. We must know what we believe and why we believe it and we must back it up with an intelligible and rational presentation. In short, what we believe and promote must be the truth, which, over the long-term, will win out.

On the other hand, not many of us are called to be "activists" by today's political definition. So let me suggest that we give serious thought to how we may have the greatest impact with the least anxiety. We can write and we can talk, but the Word of God guarantees that the biggest impression we make on the world around us will be through how we live and in the example we set. Of course, that always brings us back to the "fruits" of living and walking in the Spirit. Kinder and gentler people will produce a kinder, gentler nation.

The second group of "untouchables" is the crime and drug cartel. We must not confuse this group with common street and neighborhood criminals. How did we ever come to the point where crime touches all of our personal lives so intimately? Almost all of us have had some personal experience with crime and if we haven't, ourselves, surely our friends or family have. The boldness and audacity of these individuals is unbelievable. Our older, next door neighbors in Florida were sleeping in the supposed security of their home when "cat burglars" entered by slitting the screen on the porch. They actually entered the bedroom. They stole money and wallets without even waking up the man and his wife. In terms of the anxiety that this produced for this couple, for weeks afterward they kept every shade in the house down, even during the daytime. The lost money was of little consequence compared with the residue of fear and worry they suffered. Where once crime and criminals were a rarity, we have learned to live with the trauma of personal and vicarious experiences as portrayed and reported on television.

Crime, and particularly drugs, are really "people," greedy men and women willing to exchange human lives and even the future of our country for big bucks. In neighboring countries, they have moved into government and business, and even here they can "launder" money and operate "legitimate" businesses as a front. They can kill cops, bribe and scare witnesses, and walk out on exorbitant bail to continue their despicable work with hardly an interruption. Some of the neighborhoods of our largest cities are terrorized and run by street gangs. Organized crime can reach out into rural areas and hamlets to put a contract on anyone they target.

When I was a Chaplain at the Vermont State prison there was an inmate named Perkins who had been transferred from the Walpole State Prison in Massachusetts for protection. A very talented artist, it seems that the mob had enlisted him to make counterfeit money. When the authorities finally caught up to him, he "fingered" some of the key players in the syndicate. As a result, a contract was put out for him. Perkins confided in me that he was a "dead man," and that eventually, the mob would get him. Well, the years passed and I next met Perkins at the Veterans' Hospital where he was being treated for a heart condition prior to his release from prison. Several months later, his body turned up in the cemetery of Royalton, Vermont.

The connection between the Supreme Court and the other

"untouchables" is not physical but very real. It is "freedom." I believe there are two sides to freedom. One is the "freedom to" and the other should be "freedom from." Freedom to commit crime and go free or freedom from crime. Freedom to produce and distribute vicious anti-social, anti-feminine pornography or freedom from it and its destructive elements. A good illustration is that of pornographic bumper stickers. I believe it was Louisiana that solved this problem. A pornographic bumper sticker would be legal as long as the lettering was not more than one-eighth of an inch high. In that way, the porno-driver could proclaim his dirty message. The rest of us would need a magnifying glass to read it.

Unfortunately and amazingly, our "untouchable court" almost always seems to come down on the side of the other "untouchables." Interpretations of the first amendment would be laughable if they weren't so demoralizing. Those of us who take these things seriously are kidding ourselves if we don't detect the results of mental and ultimately physical trauma in our lives over these events.

To me, it is doubtful that anything other than massive relentless public outrage and action can stem this tide. The tide is coming in and has reached our shores. In our neighboring countries, private citizens as well as elected officials dare not speak out lest they become a morgue statistic. It is even doubtful that there is a single citizen of our own country who would be safe should these bosses decide that they were worth the price of a contract. Some even live in fear of our own government, due to their dissent and the increasing ability of the FBI or Homeland Security to target them as suspect.

The third group of "untouchables" consists of the entertainment industry, and for purposes of discussion we need to separate it into two parts: Hollywood and Television. First, consider the power of Hollywood. It probably influences the social, moral, and spiritual life of our country (and possibly the world) more than all the churches and religions put together. And Hollywood revels in fantasy.

To understand the power of Hollywood, one need go no further than this week's TV guide or an online guide to cable or satellite videos to peruse the list of movies for the week. The fare for this week and every week to come will be extreme violence, explicit sex, strong language, and adult themes. Of course these films will produce big bucks for the producers and actors, but what else will they produce?

Some knowledgeable people think that in the 1950s, a conscious and deliberate decision was made by the industry bosses to pull out all the stops and go for it, in terms of unrestricted sex and violence and even the promotion of homosexuality as an acceptable lifestyle. Self-censorship was abandoned in favor of a meaningless rating system, one that says to every thinking young person, "It's okay for adults to be naughty, but not for you."

The result was exactly what the promoters wanted. The children and youth portion of the market for "R" and "X" rated film skyrocketed as did the money lining the pockets of the industry.

With ever increasing boldness, the "untouchables" of Hollywood have become the purveyors of filth, unimaginable, a short time ago. They have done so without regard for the social consequences, and they have certainly helped to reap a bumper crop of violence, drug and alcohol addiction, casual and irresponsible sex leading to AIDS and abortion and much more. I read once that pornography on film has now become the biggest single export of our nation. It is for good reason that we are anathema to many of the peoples of the world, some of whom have become our sworn enemies for this and other reasons. Make no mistake about it, these developments have a very real and personal impact on our lives as seniors!

The real tragedy of all this is that there are great producers and actors in Hollywood and theirs could be such a tremendous contribution to a world so desperately in need of role models and moral encouragement. Occasionally, such a film appears and, amazingly enough, films like that are usually money makers. For the most part though, the cameras are spewing out more and more trash from horrible mutilation to gross sexual perversion. One article in TV Guide predicted that in the very near future, even the networks would be showing "full frontal nudity."

"You are what you eat," in relation to Hollywood means that what they produce is gobbled down and digested by great numbers of our young people and children, helping to produce the grisly results in society today. But, because the barons of Hollywood have become untouchable, common decent men and women need not raise a voice in alarm because they will not be heard. If they do, they will be vilified publicly as self-appointed censors!

Let me list things that are especially alien to me in today's lifestyle. Number one is the abortion of normal fetuses before birth, and abandoned and abused children after birth. What has happened to the mothers of our time? Even animals, birds, and fish care for and provide for their offspring until they can survive on their own. It is hard for me to accept that many of the same women who are environmentalists and would fight for whales or baby seals will kill their own offspring in the name of choice.

Secondly, the language of today is alien to me. We hear two- and three-year-olds and up using words that at best are garbage and at worst are vicious and provocative "restroom wall" words. I don't think we'll ever have a "kinder, gentler" nation as long as we have this ignorant, disgusting language.

Back to television. This industry poses one of the greatest threats to freedom because of its fantastic power to influence and control ideas. We have an excellent example of this in China today. The party bosses there used television, not only to spy on their own people, but to change and erase actual historical events. To think that millions of people sit in their own homes each day and night, letting the writers, directors, and editors of a fantasy world subtly shape their opinions and lifestyle.

One of the greatest deceptions of the last twenty-five years was the great feature, the "in" thing - couples living together having casual sex without marriage, without love, and without commitment. Just walk into a bedroom with an attractive man or woman, and sex is next. No preliminaries, no aftermath, just pleasure. At one point, it almost seemed bizarre for any intelligent, sophisticated woman or man to consider a courtship without sex and a lifelong heterosexual marriage relationship. There is hardly a program that depicts a normal father, mother, child relationship. It is a genuine miracle that, in spite of the continual negative harangue against traditional marriage, it has not only survived, but also is making a significant comeback.

As seniors, our response to this tremendous challenge must be positive in nature. Those of us fortunate enough to have a Christian partner must demonstrate to younger couples, and as yet unmarried young people, today that a lifelong marriage commitment is a precious treasure. We must display happiness, courage, romance, and the excitement of living together with Christ and most of all, true love and satisfaction. We must display publicly a Christ-like affection for those we love. We must show, not only the "rightness" of this decision but also the completeness of it. In other words, it must be attractive to those coming after.

The continuing saga of violent, irresponsible lifestyle has become a self-fulfilling prophecy, a contributing factor to broken homes by the millions, abandoned children, and neighborhoods held hostage by gang warfare and drug pushers and users, killing and being killed. A good example of this occurred during a recent excellent documentary, which I personally witnessed on a local TV channel, discussing teenage alcoholism and suicide. I could hardly believe my eyes when the program was interrupted by one of the most disgusting of beer commercials, a "light up the night" commercial depicting the joys of a "wild" and promiscuous night life. While the program was saying "no" to that lifestyle, the commercial was saying "yes" and go for it, to the very teenagers the program was designed to help.

The real danger of these morally and spiritually barren formats is not only the implication that a few executives can portray life in our nation in the twisted way they want, but more importantly that we "little people" can do nothing about it except to turn it off. Turning it off, though, in the long run may have some effect! If only the network executives would recognize from the long, consistent decline in viewers that there are still millions of us out there who would like to see and hear exciting and realistic programs without the unnecessarily offensive language and overdone sexual themes.

Television and movies are undeniably an important part of the other side of life and we as Christian seniors can and must learn to judge what effect they have on our lives.

Let me make a suggestion, which I suspect many have already done. I'm sure that we all have favorite shows and special events, which we enjoy. There is however, a whole schedule of shows that raise a pertinent question for those who love the Lord. It is, "Does this program trouble me because of its content?" Even more important, "Is it offensive to the Holy Spirit?" We can help solve this problem by putting the various shows in one of three categories, depending upon their effect on our lives: positive, passive, and negative. If we can watch a program in good conscience and it contains mostly uplifting or inspiring messages, we have no problem.

To the elderly, shut-ins and disabled, television is a major contributor to their daily life and as such has the potential to provide them with laughter and entertainment. There are a whole group of programs that I see as falling into the "passive" category. These can be news, sports, comedies, special events, music and dramas - a whole array of acceptable choices. These have not much, if any, effect on our lives spiritually, but they can make a major contribution to the happiness of our retirement life.

There is another program group that the mature Christian will make the decision not to watch. The real issue is: What does that program do to your love for Christ? Some of these shows are humorous and interesting, but contain material that is deliberately included to appeal to the side of life that is definitely not Christian. Our Bible says, "Flee youthful lusts, which war against the soul."

If a program damages your relationship to Christ and you recognize its effect, it would be much better to skip it. It is important to remind ourselves of the continuing and constant presence of the Holy Spirit in our lives, and to remember that He is sensitive to the "ingredients" of our lives, including what we watch on TV.

Ephesians 5:3-4, 4:30 say, "But among you there must not be even a hint of sexual immorality or of any kind of immorality or of any kind of impurity or of greed because these are improper for God's holy people. Nor should there be obscenity, foolish talk or coarse joking which are out of place, but rather thanksgiving. And do not grieve the Holy Spirit of God with whom you were sealed for the day of redemption."

Some time ago, the Supreme Court decided that we cannot outlaw "Dial-a-porn," even though it might have harmful effects upon the children and youth who use it. This is even worse now that our telephones have become miniature TV sets, transmitting and receiving pictures from any source.

Is there anything more important for us as Christians and as seniors than to be setting an example of purity and holiness in a world which doesn't even understand the meaning of these words? When you tune in a professional football game, you may hear the commentator use the term "momentum." Scientifically, momentum is defined as "quantity of motion." It is determined by the length of time required to bring a mass to a stop when it is under the action of a constant force.

As Christians and especially as mature Christians we must put on the brakes. We describe sports' momentum in sort of a metaphysical way. One team is driving the ball down the field, the crowd is cheering, momentum is building, the quarterback is back to pass, and he sees a receiver in the end zone. At the last instant, a defensive back steps in and intercepts the ball and runs it out to mid field. The drive is stopped, the momentum is gone.

Friends, we must stop the momentum of a "crooked and perverse" world, and demonstrate that amidst all the turmoil, trusting in the Lord can bring peace in one's inner being. Psalm 107:23-31, which the Pilgrims read aloud when they landed at Plymouth in 1620, says, "Those who go down to the sea in ships, who do business on great waters; they have seen the works of the LORD, and His wonders in the deep. For He spoke and raised up a stormy wind, which lifted up the waves of the sea. They rose up to the heavens, they went down to the depths; Their soul melted away in their misery. They reeled and staggered like a drunken man, and were at their wits' end. Then they cried to the LORD in their trouble, and He brought them out of their distresses. He caused the storm to be still, so that the waves of the sea were hushed. Then they were glad because they were quiet, so He guided them to their desired haven. Let them give thanks to the LORD for His loving kindness, and for His wonders to the sons of men."

Questions for individual or group use may be found in the Appendix, which begins on Page 141.

8

THUNDER AND LIGHTNING

I remember one time, I believe it was in 1950, that I was in the middle of a strong hurricane in Milford, Connecticut. During the full fury of the storm, entire trees were uprooted and branches were falling everywhere. Wind driven rain was assaulting the house, electric lines were down everywhere burning and shooting sparks in every direction. The storm was at its height! Where was I? Down by the shore taking pictures of the raging sea. Not a smart place to be during a hurricane. Somewhere I still have those pictures and every so often, I drag them out and try to re-imagine the roaring of the surf and the waves of mist swept up by the roiling seas. Standing there in that storm was exhilarating; it made me feel almost immortal. But that was in my youth!

Through the years we learn from experiences that there are dangers all around us, even some dangers that we never see or hear. Some of us learn how to handle dangers and others don't. When we don't know how to handle them, they turn into fears and fears left unchecked can grow into phobias. Then, we find our lives being profoundly affected. There are common fears and some that are not so common, but we are probably going to be affected by one or more during our later years. It is likely that we, ourselves, or someone close to us will experience great fears in the near future.

Several years ago, I was to perform a wedding and having set the date we proceeded to talk with the bride and groom about the particulars. In the conversation, it came out that the bride's mother would probably not attend the ceremony. However, it was not clear to me why not, since apparently it was an otherwise normal family situation.

After the wedding rehearsal, the bride's father took me aside and told me the story. In the early days of their marriage and toward the end of her first pregnancy the mother had been shopping in a large department store. In an unusual situation, the baby began to come without warning and there was no choice but to give birth right there on the floor of the store. She experienced tremendous embarrassment as ordinary shoppers stopped to gawk at the birth and, though it was not apparent at the time, she experienced great emotional trauma. Without counseling and as the years passed this woman began to socially withdraw until, even though she was relatively young, she would rarely, if ever, leave her home. This was my first experience with agoraphobia.

Fear of any kind, and particularly those that overcome us, rob our lives of their fullness and contribute to the disengagement of our life from the real world. God understands and wants to help! Fear of flying, fear of water, fear of people, closed places, enemies, sickness, and death! Are we going to let fears control our lives and rob us of happiness?

In a previous chapter, we talked about demons, part of the spirit world. The other part of the spirit world is angels and we are taught that one of their responsibilities is to care for and guard those of us who are Christians. Psalm 34:7 says, "The angel of the Lord encamps around those who fear him, and he delivers them." Hebrews 1:14 says, "Are not all angels ministering spirits sent to serve those who will inherit salvation?"

The world of angels is not "the wonderful world of Disney." The fact that we have guardian angels does not motivate us to do senseless things. When I am playing golf and it begins to thunder and lightning, I'm not supposed to hold my metal putter up in the air and challenge the lightning to hit me. Nor should I expect protection if I deliberately race wildly down the highway, ignoring the speed limit during an icy snowstorm. But there are times when the angels do intervene!

In the earlier days of my ministry, a family had come to know Christ and wanted to attend prayer meeting on Wednesday evenings. Living far out in the country and needing transportation, I decided to pick them up and take them home each week. On this particularly black night, I was on my way up the dark, twisting road to their house. I was traveling at the speed limit, but as I approached a hairpin curve and was looking directly into a wooded area, I noticed in those moments, a red reflector type light, which I had not seen before. My immediate reaction was to slow down. As I rounded the curve, there in the middle of the road was a car stalled and completely in the dark. The driver was standing in front of the car with the hood up. I barely avoided hitting him.

I haven't told this story often, nor have I embellished it. I did go back and could not find that light. I know that the angels were involved in the experience. It is probable that most of us who are true believers have experienced angels or their protecting ministry "unawares." Yet, I feel that confidence in the presence of God's ministers is more important than featuring these experiences as an enticement to live the Christian life. But they surely are one of the provisions He makes to allay the fears of our life.

1 John 1:5 says, "God is Light, in Him there is no darkness at all." 1 John 4:18 says, "There is no fear in love but perfect love drives out fear."

Isaiah 12:2 says, " Surely God is my salvation. I will trust and not be afraid. The Lord is my strength and my song;
He has become my salvation."

I am not advocating going out of your house in the middle of a storm and shouting up to the angry sky, "Lightning, go ahead and hit me," but I am advocating coming out from under your bed because your fears have gripped you and controlled you in the past and you cannot seem to overcome them. Let Jesus' words counsel you, "Let not your heart be troubled, neither let it be afraid."

We can respect danger and take precautions to be safe from it. This is not a lack of faith. However, there are times when God, in His way, will intervene to protect us when there is no other way. We use our common sense, we act rationally, we drive safely, we take care of our health, and we trust Him beyond all that.

Just outside of Melbourne, Florida, along Route 1 there used to be a huge billboard declaring something like this: "Melbourne has not had a major hurricane in fifty years." All along the outer sand dunes highway, called Route A1A, thousands of homes, businesses, and condominiums had been built, some of them with foundations below sea level. Everyone felt secure until September 2004, when in the space of twenty-two days *two* hurricanes struck, one directly and another forty-five miles south, both with winds over one-hundred miles per hour. The devastation was staggering, of biblical proportion, really, since Jesus warned of the dangers of building one's house upon sand.

Though we as Christians need not fear, we must be aware of both the danger and the victory. 1 Peter 5:8-9 says, "Be self-controlled and alert. Your enemy the devil prowls around like a roaring lion looking for someone to devour. Resist him, standing firm in your faith, because you know that your brothers throughout the world are undergoing the same kind of sufferings."

Because it does not seem that we have been attacked it doesn't mean danger and enemies are not there. They are near, lurking nearby, but so is the Lord and so is all the protection we will ever need. Like David, we can sit down at the "table of God" and have a banquet even with the unseen enemies about! Psalm 23:5 exclaims, "You prepare a table before me in the presence of my enemies. You anoint my head with oil. My cup overflows."

Questions for individual or group use may be found in the Appendix, which begins on Page 141.

9

UNITARIANS, FIRE, AND PERSONAL INTEGRITY

I was pastoring a Baptist church in a Vermont community. Right across the street and next to our parsonage was a white Unitarian church. It seemed to me that all the wealthy, influential people of the town were somehow divided up between the Congregational and Unitarian churches, depending upon the degree of their liberality. In my pastoral adolescence, I had some strange ideas about how God works, and I had some very distinctly negative feelings about that church. Don't get me wrong, I liked the people of the congregation, but the doctrine was particularly offensive to me. One particular pastor, at the ecumenical clergy meetings, took great pleasure in trodding under foot our sacred beliefs. For example, his idea of communion was that Jesus was just down at the local pub having a snifter with the local boozers, one of the "good old boys"!

Well, one day during a violent thunderstorm, lightning struck the steeple of that white church. I felt sure that God was either issuing a warning or beginning a time of judgment. After all, a church that thought that "the brotherhood of man and the Fatherhood of God" was too strong a doctrine had to be on the bad side of God. That was until something happened to the brick church on the other side of the street - mine!

I was up at the Fairgrounds playing third base in the Men's softball league, wearing a kelly green uniform, trimmed in gold, replete with the name of a local hardware store, our sponsor, on the back.

In about the third inning, the fire whistle at the downtown

fire station went off with a long whining sound. I thought it must be the Unitarian church! At that precise moment, one of my church deaconesses came barreling into the park in her car, jumped out, running up to me and saying, "Pastor our church is on fire! Hurry!"

Well, it was and I did!

In the local paper the next day was a picture of the "Reverend" being interviewed in front of the church. The kelly green was covered with black soot, as was my face and entire body. What looked to be tears were running down my face. The caption under the photograph went something like this: "Pastor rescues sacred treasures from church during the fire."

Actually, all I did was take out the pulpit Bible and a few hymnbooks. The "tears" were really sweat drops from the heat. I really wasn't a hero at all!

But that fire did teach me a lesson. For one thing, the fire turned out to be a blessing in disguise for our church. It pulled the congregation together in a special kind of unity. As a result, we were able to completely redecorate and renovate the building, mostly with insurance money.

The other lesson was about "spiritual integrity." I needed to pull together some of my wild doctrinal ideas and bring them into conformity with what the Bible really taught. From that time on I would let God decide who needed to judged and taught lessons. I decided that my own spiritual integrity was the most important issue of my life. I am glad that God didn't make me a judge instead of a pastor!

There is nothing more devastating in life than self-deception. Theologically, it is not contradictory to say that there are two aspects to the subject of sinless perfection. The Scriptures indicate that Jesus Christ is the "propitiation" for our sins. In that sense, God the Father can look upon us and see us as sinless through His own Son.

1 John 1:7 says, "But if we walk in the light as He is in the light, we have fellowship with one another and the blood of Jesus, His Son purifies us from all sin."

Yet, in the very next verse, John writes, "If we claim to be without sin, we deceive ourselves and the truth is not in us."Personal "integrity" is the will to do the right thing when we are alone, away from peer pressures, in some cases, alone with only ourselves as witnesses, or when we are keeping company with non-Christians. Integrity for the child or young person will come from his or her commitment to Christ, the input from his family and church, and the principles he has learned and accepted. It will be at that point when temptation and opportunity to sin or break the law are present that his integrity will either succeed or fail. And so it is with older Christians as well. To do the right thing - what a simple expectation from a caring, loving God!

Micah 6:8 says, "He has showed you, O man what is good. And what does the Lord require of you? To act justly, and to love mercy and to walk humbly with your God."

Integrity is especially important to me because it concerns a certain inner confidence I have in myself, based upon my love for Christ.

As we grow older and the nature of our role in life becomes more toward counseling and teaching, the experiences we have had can be most helpful, both to ourselves and to others. We have all discovered "how to" and "how not to" handle situations. One of Webster's definitions for integrity is "moral soundness, honesty, and uprightness." I discovered that my spiritual integrity revolves around my belief in God and the application of His Word to my life.

Some years ago, as a pastor, I was faced with a situation and a decision that was mine alone to handle. A young man, a member of my congregation had just completed his Navy career and returned home. He and some others had attended a bachelor party and were returning home in an open jeep. As they rounded a bend in the country road and were coming down a steep hill, somehow the driver lost control and they ran over an embankment and into a gully. This young man was thrown from the jeep and headlong into a birch tree. His body was completely broken from head to foot - fractured skull, ribs, lungs, and legs. The accident had a particularly devastating effect upon his family, since he was an only child. Taken to a local medical center, he hung in there and somehow survived over eight hours of surgery.

On the second evening he took a definite turn for the worse. I was at home eating supper when I received the call. It was his grandmother, who was one of our church's deaconesses. The conversation went something like this, "Pastor, my grandson is unconscious and the hospital has notified his parents to come up immediately because he is sinking. I'm asking you, on his behalf, to go up and anoint him with oil and pray that his life well be spared."

Of course my answer was "Yes." Not having time to prepare, I took some ordinary cooking oil in a small container, jumped into the car and was on my way. I had driven a short distance up the highway when suddenly I realized that I personally had reached a "crisis" point in my life. I pulled over and, in a few moments, thought about a lot of things, but the bottom line was this. I knew well the promise of God's Word in the book of James concerning the saving of a life and I felt that the conditions of the verse had been met. James 5:14 says, "Is any sick among you? Let him call for the elders of the church; and let them pray over him, anointing him with oil in the name of the Lord: and the prayer of faith shall save the sick; and if he has committed sins, they shall be forgiven him" (King James Version).

In these verses, I see two main conditions and a process. First there must be an act of faith to "call for the elders" and secondly, there must be a "prayer of faith" offered. The act of obedience or process is "anointing him with oil in the name of the Lord." If and when these conditions are met, we then believe the promise of God for healing and forgiveness.

But did I have the personal integrity to believe? That was a turning point in my life and ministry, because it brought into dramatic focus for me the issue of my faith and how real it was. In those moments, my career as a pastor was at issue; my whole Christian commitment of faith was before me. There were no lights or other special effects, but in that car, beside that road, I found that I did have spiritual integrity, I did believe God!

I continued to the hospital believing that the Lord was going to do a miracle. Entering the Intensive Care Unit, I found the young man, unconscious, his vital signs slowly slipping. In a simple act of faith, I anointed him with oil, and prayed the prayer that had come out of my experience, a prayer for the sparing of his life. He could not hear and no change was immediately apparent. His parents had not yet arrived, but I believe that by the time they did come, he had rallied and had begun the first phase of recovery. The story does have a happy ending because he went on to fully recover and marry. It was an experience that had a profound effect upon my life.

The real test of our spiritual integrity comes, not when there is a miracle or healing, but when the conditions seem right for one, and yet it doesn't happen. Now the experience above strengthened my faith and confirmed the promises of God's Word. Since then, however, I have had to be reminded that although God can intervene to change the natural course of events, He doesn't always do so. I received an emergency call sometime later, a similar circumstance. A young man, a teenager had been swimming in a local brook with a group of friends. He dove off a bridge, hitting his head on the bottom, and had sustained a severe neck injury. It was determined at the hospital that his spinal column had been severed and he was losing his spinal fluid, a situation which is almost always fatal. I thus became involved in another situation that tested my faith in a number of ways.

As I drove up to the boy's home that night and stopped outside the house, I had no idea what to say. The family were not church people and I wondered if they had any special faith at all for the crisis. As I knocked on the door, I still wondered what I could possibly say or do to help these folks. The door opened and I was welcomed in. I knew the family from our activities in Little League. The Holy Spirit moved me to put my arm around the distraught mother and dad and I simply said something about the Lord loving and caring for them.

At a sensitive moment like that, it would be easy to "blow"

the whole situation and turn a whole family away from the Lord and produce anger and hostility, instead of receptiveness. I didn't say much more but I assured them that the Lord cared for their son, Jeff, and would be with them through it all.

That became to me another test case for my faith because the other miraculous healing was still fresh in my mind. I reasoned that if this boy were healed of an impossible situation, it would be a fantastic testimony to the whole community and would lead to the salvation of many people. The focus I had on healing became almost an obsession. I began to make demands of God, not in a bold way, but in a sort of bargaining way. I felt I had good reason to ask for a genuine miracle.

I visited Jeff, often. One of the most heart-rending aspects of his condition was that, though his life was slowly ebbing away, he was totally conscious. I talked to Jeff about his soul, although I did not use his condition as a bargaining chip. We talked about life and about what Jesus had done for us on the cross. I found him very receptive and after several conversations, Jeff responded by giving his heart to Christ. This reinforced my belief that God was going to heal him.

It was during the summer months, and I was due to go to Connecticut for our vacation. Since Jeff's condition was not changing rapidly, my youth leader persuaded me to go - he would look after Jeff. One night about a week later, I found myself at about midnight very troubled and my thoughts were on Jeff. I decided to do something I had only done once before, to pray and study the Bible until I had an answer. After a period of deep prayer and emotionally straining thought, my eyes fell on a portion of Scripture that was open before me. At first, I didn't fully comprehend what the Lord was saying, because, although the Bible is God's Word, it does not always speak so directly and specifically to a given situation. If it had not been for all of the "ingredients" in that setting, I might even have been a bit afraid. It was such a direct, specific answer from God!

My eyes first fell on John 11:14, "Then said Jesus unto them, Lazarus is dead." God had spoken to me, but He had more to say.

"Jesus said unto her, I am the resurrection and the life, he that believeth in me, though he were dead, yet shall he live, and whosoever believeth in me shall never die. Believest thou this?"

Before I received the phone call from my youth leader a few minutes later, I knew that Jeff had died physically. But the whole issue of life and death and my own spiritual integrity had again come to a climax. This time victory was not in the miraculous sparing of a life but in the deepest sensitivity to the Word of God and the teaching, comforting ministry of the Holy Spirit, and especially in the glorious truth of Jesus' words. Jeff, in truth, was not dead after all, but with the Lord. This, friends is the very bottom line of our Christian faith.

Perhaps the greatest test of our spiritual integrity comes in regard to our own personal health or safety. Let me illustrate this by recounting several experiences, each related to my health and each having a spiritual impact on my life. First, however, let's consider the example of Paul, the Apostle. If there were ever a man worthy of God's special "treatment" it would be Paul. He had done everything asked of him in God's service and suffered the consequences. In human terms he had earned a special place in the church and, we would think, in the plan of God. He had every right to claim the promises of the Word of God concerning health and long life. Yet Paul was a very sick man. Daily he had to contend with failing eyesight, a body full of wounds and broken bones, continual pain. What's more, he prayed at least three times specifically that God would heal him and his motivation was that he might better serve. In other words, all the right conditions seemed present - the deserving man, the hurting body, and the right motivation. But it didn't happen! Why not? It was not that God did not answer Paul's prayer, because He did. Witness 2 Corinthians 12:7-10: "To keep me from becoming conceited because of these surpassingly great revelations, there was given me a thorn in my flesh, a messenger from Satan, to torment me. Three times I pleaded with the Lord to take it away from me. But He said to me, 'My Grace is sufficient for you, for my power is made perfect in weakness.' Therefore, I will boast all the more gladly about my weaknesses, so that Christ's power may rest on me. That is why, for Christ's sake, I delight in weaknesses, in insults, in hardships, in persecutions, in difficulties. For when I am weak, then am I strong."

Some years ago, we were in the process of building Singing Hills Retreat Center and because we had little money, we were doing it with our own lumber and volunteer labor. For me, it was heavy, demanding work and I found myself suffering from a double hernia, the result of heavy lifting at a summer camp several years before. The doctor had indicated that the condition was not severe enough for surgery, but would grow worse with the passing of time.

I felt very enthusiastic about the current project, but I was troubled and handicapped by my health situation. One evening, I was sitting in the living room or our home, looking out over the hills of New Hampshire. Although beautiful and inspirational, it was not a particularly spiritual setting. Yet, the Lord put a "seed faith" thought in my mind and it was this, "I know God can heal that hernia so that I can continue this project for Him." Again, there were no special effects, no wind, no warm feeling, but I was healed. It was a very simple event!

Now, years later I am still healed of the hernias, but I have another health problem that is a cause for anxiety, not so much because it is severe or terminal but it is to me a "thorn in the flesh." I have made this a matter of testing for myself. Yet I wonder if I, and many other Christians, are not beset by a kind of spiritual "delusion of grandeur," a sort of physical perfectionism that expects that as a Christian I ought to be totally free of any bodily weaknesses or diseases. The options for me are pretty simple. Either God intervenes and heals me, I continue to live with the condition, or I must have a moderately serious operation.

There is another question that we must answer. Since God is involved in our lives and since He is concerned with our health and well-being, is a defect in our body something He permitted or is it a "messenger" from Satan? In either case, it is apparent that IT IS A MESSAGE! If it is from Satan, we can assume that it is his way of hurting us spiritually with fear or anxiety. If it is from God, we can assume from the teaching of Paul that its purpose is to give us strength. And once again, the bottom line is personal integrity in my relationship to God. In fact, in both cases the purpose of the message is to strengthen my faith. For as the Bible exhorts,"Resist the devil and he will flee from you."

In the later years of our life, nothing is more important to us than our relationship with God the Father. You may know the hymn that says, "Turn your eyes upon Jesus, look full in His wonderful face, and the things of earth will grow strangely dim, in the light of His glory and grace."

An old proverb says, "You can't teach an old dog new tricks." Related to us as seniors, it obviously means we are so stubborn and set in our ways that we can't adapt. I'd like to dispute that and suggest a new proverb that goes like this, "Old dogs can learn new tricks and new dogs can learn old tricks." That's where our new teaching and counseling role comes in. For us there are many Scriptures that talk about "new" and "newness" for our lives. For example, Romans 12:2 says, "And be not conformed to this world but be transformed by the renewing of your mind, that you may prove what is that good, and acceptable, and perfect, will of God." This verse is in no way associated with age. Not only is it possible but it is absolutely essential that we continue to learn. Lessons from the past can teach new dogs old tricks. For example, there is the question of "what to say" in a difficult situation or in seeking to share your faith. Now, there is a promise about this! The promise is that, if, and when, we're "lost" for words, the Holy Spirit will tell us what to say and in effect, speak through us.

I experienced this at a prison Christmas party! As Chaplain it was my responsibility to pick an inmate committee to plan and produce the annual Christmas party. In the preliminary meeting it was decided that the main feature of the party would be a local "county-western" band called "Woody and the Ramblers." In addition, there would be the traditional carol singing, a few remarks by me, and then cake and ice cream to top it off! Doesn't that sound simple?

This was to be a Christmas party I would never forget! After some minor squabbling among the committee members, everything was set and the day came for the party. Together with the inmate committee and Woody and the Ramblers, I was in the chapel putting the finishing touches on my remarks. At about that same time a "rumble" was beginning in the cell blocks. Now, some "rumbles" are worse than others and this one fell somewhere between bad and not so bad. The "cons" were sure making enough noise banging pans and other available items on the cell bars and yelling as loud as they could.

Woody, the band leader, was a very big man, about a size 48, but I could see that he and the other band members were getting jittery. Actually, our location wasn't very reassuring either - the chapel in the ancient prison was located above the kitchen in a very flammable wooden structure, replete with the grease from over a hundred years of cooking. The question of the moment became whether to have the party or to cancel it, a decision that only the Warden could make. He decided that the "show must go on."

So, here we are, the committee, Woody and his group, and myself up on the stage as over 300 "Maximum Security" inmates begin to file into the chapel, accompanied by eight unarmed guards and the associate warden ... and I am in charge (so to speak!). The men are still up tight and there is grumbling and some shouting, and as the associate warden comes in there is booing, which was totally undeserved since he had initiated many reforms for the men since his arrival, including the right to watch TV each evening.

As I prepare to get up to the microphone, I appraise the situation. We're supposed to be having a party, but we've got over 300 unhappy men on our hands, a very nervous band, and I'm not exactly comfortable myself. In fact, I haven't got the slightest idea how to handle the situation, but I do remember the promise of God's Word to give me wisdom and the very real assistance of the Holy Spirit.

To this day, I don't remember what I did say, only that it was something like this, "Men, we've been planning this party for you for a long time and we're here to have a good time in the spirit of Christmas. I hope you can find it in your hearts to make it a good time for all of us."

Having said that, I quickly turned to Woody and asked him to "strike up the band." After the first few bars, the men broke into clapping and singing and the crisis was over. I truly believe that the Lord had given me special words to speak for a special situation.

There is a brief postscript to this story. After the party and cake and ice cream were being served, I noticed a young man standing by the windows wistfully looking out into the barren "yard." As I drew near, I noticed that there were tears in his eyes and since I knew Paul from counseling, I asked if I could help. He was a handsome and intelligent young man; his crime had not been of a violent nature. He just stood there and said, "I just don't know how this happened to me. I just wish I could be home for Christmas. Paul was one of the minority of inmates who later went on to make a success of their lives.

In my proverb about "old dogs doing old tricks and new dogs learning old tricks," I'm really talking about experience and "technique." We as seniors have extremely valuable information to share with our younger counterparts. In this case the lesson concerns how to handle a "sticky" situation using the resources that God has promised in His Word, wisdom, courage, and, most of all, the help of the Holy Spirit.

One of the great lessons we can share with others is "how to laugh at ourselves" and of course we learn this from experience. Witness this scenario: I am in the pulpit as usual on Sunday morning midway through the service. Now, although I am not ritualistic in nature, there are certain formalities that I go through in conducting a worship service. One of those is to blow my nose and clear my throat during the offertory while I am sitting down behind the pulpit and out of sight from the congregation.

On this particular Sunday the choir was standing directly behind me as I proceeded to pull out my handkerchief from my rear pocket in order to blow my nose. Early that morning, I had gone to my bureau drawer, as usual, reached in and taken the neatly folded handkerchief and put it into my pocket. The only thing is that as I gingerly took the handkerchief in my fingers and flicked it out to open it, instead of a handkerchief, out dropped one of my wife's white nurse's stockings, which proceeded to fall full length and in full view of the choir and the congregation.

I am frozen for a moment, not knowing what to do and not daring to look around at the choir because I know they had witnessed the whole event. I can hear the undertone of laughter. Well, I found it's best to use the fun of the moment to your advantage and almost without exception, embarrassing moments can be turned into great illustrations. So I stand up, display the stocking to the congregation, and quickly think of something to say. Again, thank you Holy Spirit!

I believe that some of the humorous experiences of our lives are really gems of great value. They provide us with subjects for lots of laughs and good conversation, and they become even more important as we grow older. A part of our lives that provides us with perhaps the most pleasure of all is getting together with Christian friends and sharing stories that we can all identify with. Not only is this the best entertainment, but it is free. So be thankful when something funny happens to you.

While we're on the subject of "old dogs learning new tricks" let me tell you about "Sandy," our collie. While the children were growing up we had a series of dogs of every kind. Some were extremely smart and easy to be trained and some got left out when brains were dispensed. For example, we had one Labrador Retriever who knew just which items of clothing to bring home from the neighbor's clothesline. Another one, a mutt, was regularly found standing on all fours in the middle of the kitchen table eating out of the sugar bowl. There was Andy, Candy, and then came Sandy, and she could sing! If we held our head up in the air and howled, in just the right pitch, she would join in. Of course, hopefully, no one saw my entire family with their heads in the air, howling. But the crowning event happened one summer evening as I was preparing to go to bed.

Our son Paul had taken over the attic as a camping out bedroom for the summer, and it was way up on the third floor of the old parsonage. He had moved an old stuffed chair by the open window and it was there in the comfort of that chair that "Sandy" spent her summer nights, often with her front feet hanging out of the window.

We'll never know for sure, but my belief is that Sandy had a dream, perhaps envisioning that she was chasing a cat. As I was heading for the stairs to our second floor bedroom, I heard a swishing sound and saw what looked to be a ball of fur go plummeting past the window! I fully expected to see her limp body on the cement sidewalk as I rushed out the front door and around the house. To my amazement, there was Sandy standing on all fours with a very puzzled expression on her face. It seems that she had fallen those twenty or more feet and landed on the cover of the propane gas container, and had bounced off onto the ground, landing upright. Later, when the veterinarian confirmed that she had no serious injuries, we had lots of laughs. In those days of the TV series "The Flying Nun," the local newspaper carried the story of "Sandy, the Flying Dog." I think that there are many seniors who could share pet stories that would produce smiles and laughs for themselves and their friends. And laughter really is good medicine, as Proverbs 17:22 says, "A merry heart doeth good like a medicine but a broken spirit drieth the bones."

Not all of the lessons come from our own personal experience. I think one of the tests of true friendship is whether our friends can laugh at themselves and tell you about it. I don't consider myself to be selective in choosing good friends, but somehow, the ones closest to us have turned out to be folks with a good sense of humor, so the following story comes second hand.

Two of our best friends, a husband and wife, were on vacation in Florida, staying at our home there. Eating out is one of the favorite pastimes of retirees in Florida and there is an abundance of inexpensive restaurants to choose from. On this particular occasion, our friends chose a new small Chinese restaurant in a nearby shopping mall. Upon entering the lobby, our friends asked the hostess if they had a "No Smoking" area, whereupon she replied, that the restaurant was too small for that and would they mind waiting a few moments to be seated.

About that time, a rather scruffy looking little old lady appeared and was standing next to our friend, Wayne. This lady was probably well into her seventies. Wayne, my friend, had just the right knack for saying the right words, at the wrong time, so when this lady pulled out a pack of cigarettes and lit up, he said, "You don't mean to tell me, a lady like you smokes?" On this occasion, these were evidently the "right words," because the little lady looked right at Wayne and in a loud raspy voice, audible to all the restaurant patrons, said, "Yes, I do, and if you didn't eat so much, you wouldn't be so darn fat!" (Note: "darn") is my interpretation.)

There's a lesson here for all of us seniors, isn't there? Speaking for myself, the lesson is to be prepared for any response with a laugh at yourself and a smile for others. Pastors particularly are prime targets for interesting remarks. For example, early on in my ministry, of course I thought I was going to be another Billy Graham. In fact, I had heard that as a young preacher in North Carolina, he would go out in a pasture and practice preaching to the rocks, hills, and cows. I figured that whatever would work in North Carolina ought to work in New Hampshire, because we had rocks, hills, and cows too! So, when I took my first pastorate, I regularly went up on the hillside and practiced my oratory.

I was a Connecticut Yankee, and I hadn't learned the New Hampshire psyche - after all, when you have "Live Free or Die" on your state license plate there has to be something blunt and truthful about your character. So several weeks later, after delivering what I thought was a heart pounding, dynamic message, I stood at the door, greeting the parishioners as they left. One of my deacons came up, shook my hand, like he was milking a cow and said, "Pastor, I just want you to know that your sermon this morning was a lot better than last week's!"

On another occasion, I was in the midst of a wedding ceremony, this time in Vermont. You need to know that in those days, Vermont farm families always had a lot of children, I assume to help with the chores. One of the worst fates was if they kept trying and every new one turned out to be a girl. And that was particularly true a few years ago before the girls started doing most of the work. On this occasion, the ceremony was going along in great style, just as we had rehearsed. The bride and groom, with their attendants, were standing there and the bride's father was just behind her. "Who giveth this woman to be married to this man?" I asked.

"Her mother and I do." the father answered and then moved back toward his seat. However, and believe me "however" is a big word in wedding ceremonies, he stopped as he came to his pew, turned to the audience and spoke, as only a Vermont farmer can. Looking toward me, but speaking to the crowd he said, "Pastor, this is the last of my seven daughters to get hitched and am I glad"! With that he sat down.

Someone may say, "These are great stories, but what do they have to do with the 'other side of life'"? The answer lies in the humor! If we consider the impact of all the negative and demoralizing features of our lives as we grow older, we will treasure and appreciate the truly good and personal humor that comes into our lives from time to time, and we'll keep it in our memory for future reference, knowing that someday we will certainly need another laugh.

Another "old trick" that we have learned and that we can teach to the "new dogs" is "doing the impossible." Every so often we hear of really elderly people doing some remarkable physical feats, like an eighty-seven-year-old woman climbing Mt. Everest, or a ninety-year-old man parachute jumper. I had a distant cousin but we called him "Uncle" Frank, who in his later years loved to roller skate. Most of our family thought he was just a bit touched because they thought the normal thing to do at that age was to sit around and play pinochle. Secretly, I admired "Uncle" Frank, and made it my goal that if I lived to be as old as he was, I would stay active, too.

Previously I suggested that we find a happy medium between absolute boredom and bizarre antics. After all, we're past the stage where we have to prove our "macho." But some of the things we think are impossible are just over the line of possibility and we need to have the courage and imagination to cross that line from time to time. Some of us are "handcuffed" to tradition. We've never been up in a plane, never gone on a long trip, never played golf - try them, you may like them! Perhaps the state of New Hampshire has this in mind because in a dramatic spirit of generosity, they offer a free pass, not including insurance, to all the state run ski areas for senior citizens over 65.

Each of us has an area of "forbidden territory" in our lives. By that, I mean, we made the decision a long time ago that there was something in life in which we would never participate. I'm not talking about things that are right and wrong, but rather about adventures we would rather not have. With me it's the air! The air above the earth is for birds. While I have learned to "like" and even enjoy flying in the big jets, the idea of sky diving or hang gliding is still anathema to me. Height and being up in the air are definitely not my "thing." And I know that I'm missing some great thrills. Perhaps my problem with flying goes back to my earlier days as a young pastor when one of the men of my church, a pilot, invited me for a short flight around the area. He was a member of a local flying club and was an excellent pilot. We boarded the small plane after a careful maintenance check and prepared to take off. We taxied down the runway and were making a turn into the wind, when we hit a small hole in the apron of the runway and a wheel strut collapsed. This fueled my imagination as I envisioned us landing and the strut collapsing. It was also the end of our flight for that day and for some years thereafter!

Some time later, I had a youth minister who was also a licensed pilot. He had the brilliant idea that we should fly down to Boston, to Logan airport and attend a Boston Red Sox afternoon game. With the other incident still in my mind, at first I said no, but he convinced me that it would be a lot of fun and nothing to worry about. So, on the given day, I found myself airborne once again and although I was not aware of it, I guess my questions and comments finally got to him, because he said something like this, "Shut up and let me do the flying." That sealed my lips!

The flight was smooth and uneventful, until we landed at Logan. We taxied through the private part of the airport to an area where many small planes were parked. As we were approaching the empty parking area, it was necessary to make a turn, and as I looked out my side it appeared that the wing tip was going to touch the fence. I'm thinking, *Mike must know what he's doing and my lips are sealed.* "Crunch," the wing hits the fence and we're in trouble! There's a tear in the metal, but my lips are still sealed. And, we had to return home by bus and never did see the Red Sox play that day.

Now that I'm a senior, I've crossed the line again. One of my very best friends is a pilot and flies small planes. To him, flying and being up in the air comes naturally. So, when we spend some time in Florida, we rent a small plane and go for a spin. Up and down the beach we go at about a thousand feet, over the rivers and communities below. It is not only fun but also exhilarating. We come in low toward the airstrip, directly over my home and look down into the yard and neighborhood, what a beautiful sight! Maybe the air isn't just for birds, after all!

Perhaps by now you have figured out that I am trying to encourage those who are on the other side of life to try new things and to overcome fears and anxieties that have kept them "grounded" in a world that has so much to offer. When Jesus spoke to the people He often used a term "harden your neck" to define spiritual stubbornness. The opposites of such stubbornness, spiritually speaking, are openness, sensitivity, and warmth.

On a psychological level, in regard to the kind of adventurous living I am suggesting, let me call it "flexibility," which results in us doing and enjoying things that we thought were impossible. Let me illustrate with several personal experiences.

Perhaps you can identify even though you have never been a pastor, with the feelings of a young man, just out of seminary entering into a whole world of new experiences that he has only heard about in the classroom, such as marriages, funerals, and baptisms. These kinds of pastoral duties could be matched with a hundred similar challenges in other jobs and in most cases those first experiences are lonely. We wonder if we have the "stuff" it takes, as well as the courage that will be needed.

In my case, the Lord gave me the main event in my first tests. The first wedding included two couples being married and standing up for each other as best man and maid of honor, with four rings. If I could pull this off, I'd never have to worry about another wedding! I did!

Then there was the first baptism, eighteen adults in a lake including several folks over seventy who hadn't been in lake water for years. There was the lady who had asthma and another lady who was sickly and has been advised against baptism for health reasons. I respected the doctor's advice, but these people were all determined to follow our Lord's command and they had the faith to back up their decision. Aside from an apology from the elderly folks for taking Anacin prior to the baptism and some snorting, spitting, and sneezing on the part of the others, we had a most inspiring service - another duty taken care of for the next thirty-five years, except for one thing!

In my Vermont church, which I pastored years later, we had a most unusual baptistry tank. For financial reasons, the men of the church had voluntarily built it and it provided an excellent place for indoor baptisms. Being Baptist, we believed in baptism by immersion. The only thing is that as time went by, the tank began to leak and no matter what we did to fix it, the leak would run through the floor and fill up the light globe in the kitchen below. After a number of baptisms, as I waited in that kitchen below, for the beginning of the service, I could almost tell the time by the amount of water in that light globe. But, the other thing about the tank was that it was just six feet long, and on one particular occasion, I had to baptize a young man who was at least six foot six and weighed about two hundred pounds. The word that I kept thinking about, as I watched that light globe fill up with water was "flexibility," and that is the word I whispered in his ear as we went down into the water together. Bend those legs, I thought and he went down and up again - "buried with Christ in baptism, that even as Christ was raised from the dead, even so we should also walk in newness of live."

"Flexibility" and "newness of life" is really what this whole discussion is about. It is a challenge to keep expanding the parameters of your life as you grow older - to do what you thought was impossible, and to walk through the doors to potential new adventures as they open up to you.

Questions for individual or group use may be found in the Appendix, which begins on Page 141.

······· *10* ········

THE OTHER SIDE OF THE OTHER SIDE OF LIFE

Preachers, especially young ones, don't always know what to expect as a response to their messages. As a new and somewhat dogmatic young pastor, I once preached a sermon on "Home Baptists." The thrust of it concerned professing Christians who never seemed to darken the door of a church.

My text was Hebrews 10:25: "Let us not give up meeting together, as some are in the habit of doing, but let us encourage one another, and all the more as you see the day approaching."

That was in the morning service! As I entered the building for the evening service that Sunday, I encountered a man who was obviously overwrought emotionally. He was so upset that he almost required physical restraint on the part of the deacons. Approaching him, I asked, "What is the problem?"

"How dare you talk about my mother that way!" he practically shouted at me. Now this was mystifying to me, since I didn't really know him very well, nor did I know his mother at all. I discovered that he had interpreted my morning message about Home Baptists as being about his mother, who evidently never attended church.

This experience became a learning situation for me. It seems that this young man had been in a serious accident. He had a metal plate implanted in his skull and his responses were not always normal or rational. He tended to be very suspicious and imaginative, and always interpreted general statements as personal attacks upon himself or his family. It raised a very important question for me, and one that many Christians are asking today:

How do we handle the mentally afflicted when they come into our midst?

This is a particularly difficult subject to understand and discuss. There is a whole wealth of information available to Christians on the prevention of mental problems, but only a minimum available on how to handle those in our midst who are already afflicted.

This is a subject that is affecting the Body of Christ in an ever-increasing way. It probably is one of the greatest contributing factors to pastoral burnout and confusion within the churches today. I have gained some important insight in the course of more than forty years of ministry. Some of the experiences have been humorous in nature and some quite tragic. All of them, however, have had both their human side and their spiritual side and each deserved my compassion and caring. I feel sure that as we grow older, not only will we see more of this in society but also it is very likely that it will touch our lives and our churches in a personal way.

I believe that we can see in the Scriptures three distinct categories of "mind trouble," which produce bizarre or "altered behavior." First, there is "mental illness," which is physiologically initiated and which can be specifically diagnosed and in many cases treated. Second, there is what I call "self-inflicted," humanistically inspired, "altered behavior." Third, there is behavior that is directly controlled by evil spirits, which is called "demon possession."

There are many preachers today who believe and treat every case of strange or evil behavior as if it were "demon possession." I personally do not believe that this interpretation is either scriptural or reasonable. While it is a biblical fact that Satan is the author of all evil and that sin is the instrument that acts it out, both the Old and New Testaments indicate that different and significant definitions can be applied to these problems. We'll consider each of these three cases but first let's consider one of the most amazing scenarios in the whole Bible, found in the 1 Samuel 21. Imagine the future King of Israel, the "man after God's own heart," the ancestor of Jesus, scrawling graffiti on the door and deliberately drooling saliva down his beard.

1 Samuel 21:12-13 recounts, "David took these words to heart and was very much afraid of Achish, king of Gath. So he feigned insanity in their presence and while he was in their hands he acted like a madman, making marks on the doors of the gate and letting saliva run down his beard. Achish said to his servants, 'Look at this man! He is insane! Why bring him to me?'"

This unusual passage reveals several things. First, insanity is nothing new, for it obviously existed thousands of years ago. Second, it was surely not demon possession. Third, it can be either real or imitated, and last, it is characterized by unusual or bizarre behavior.

Mental illnesses that have a physiological origin are the most common and also the most tragic in their association with the Body of Christ. The reasons are quite simple, first because we don't understand them and second, because we can't accept them. Yet there is more than adequate proof that this kind of sickness not only exists but is becoming more prevalent, stimulated by the ever-mounting pressures of today's society. In many cases, doctors definitely know the cause, treatment, and prognosis for these diseases. In addition to those diagnosed, I believe there are countless others living on the very edge of these disorders. Sometimes they cross the line, and it is important that we recognize this when it happens! I feel that we as evangelical Christians have an added responsibility toward our afflicted friends because we provide a setting that is especially susceptible to emotional highs and lows. Individuals who are sensitive emotionally and spiritually are also responsive, as well they should be. The gospel itself is emotionally stimulating.

In the parable of the seed and the sower, Jesus spoke of the seed that fell on shallow ground. He likened it to the Word of God being received with joy. It sprang up but when the sun beat upon it, it died because it did not have sufficient root. I believe that we must emphasize in our preaching "high plane" living rather than "magical moment" living. The mountain peak experience must be coupled with the long, steady climb of study and growth and the resulting strong roots.

Those most vulnerable to "fantasy" Christianity are often the cream of the crop people in our churches, people who are really seeking God's will. There was such a young man in my early career as a youth pastor. This fine young man had graduated from high school and was deeply concerned about what the Lord wanted him to do for his life's work. This concern was so intense that it became a fixation, the focal point of everything he did or talked about. One day I met him and it seemed that a great load had been lifted and even his appearance was altered. From the deeply concerned, even brooding manner of recent days, he was visibly happy and obviously on a spiritual "high." He told me what had happened.

God had spoken to him in a most unusual way, in a dream or vision! He had been awakened in the middle of the night by a strange light. In each corner of his room there were lights that resembled neon signs and all of them were the same. They contained the letters MBI. The message was clear to him! God was telling him that he should attend Moody Bible Institute.

In the following days, his life became more and more characterized by trips of fantasy with events and experiences that were very real to him but in fact did not happen at all. He had crossed the line and clearly needed help.

Have you known people like that? In this case, the Lord did answer prayer and this young man found help and went on to live a productive life.

Looking back over more than forty years of ministry, I feel that there are many professing Christians living on the very edge of bipolar disorder, or schizophrenia. In the first case, they are people who live the roller coaster life of mountain peaks and valleys. When these folks are on a spiritual high, they are dynamic and highly motivated. Translated into their relationship to the church, they are great members and workers. The only trouble is they often go from one end of the spectrum to the other without any outward cause or warning. This makes the pastor or other leaders susceptible to counting on workers who have a deep problem of inconsistency. Also, they're often the most likeable, potentially successful candidates for service. With proper diagnosis and treatment with the newer, excellent drugs, these folks can function well and consistently on the higher plane of living I've described.

Then there are those living on the border of schizophrenia, a mental illness that is sometimes dubbed a split or dual personality, that is characterized by poor orientation to reality and is still an enigma to medicine. You are never quite sure who you are dealing with, or what's going on in their mind. They often have some type of paranoia similar to the young fellow who was sure I was preaching about his mother.

One thing to be careful about is opening up the "floor" of a church meeting for testimonies when a mentally disabled person is in attendance. While we must respect their disability, of which they may or may not be aware, we also need to protect the flock and especially seekers of the truth from hearing something like one person said in one of our praise times. "I thank God for my x-ray vision," he said, "so that when I am playing cards, I can see the other players' cards."

He sat down and I was rather stunned and quickly made some kind of comment. This incident, though, taught me two lessons. One was that if we want spontaneity and freedom in the worship time, we need to accompany them with some pre-stated guidelines. Secondly, we must be up front about the problem. Although this young man was never totally healed of his disease, I can testify to the fact that many times as he sat in the congregation I could sense that he was about to have a seizure, which would probably disrupt the service. I silently prayed for him, and almost without exception the seizure seemed to lessen and became manageable. Later, I learned to say to the congregation, "This young man has epilepsy and he needs our prayer and support. We care about him." That was how I stated the case.

So, without doubt, there are physiologically induced mental disabilities, including those mentioned above, plus diseases of aging such as Alzheimer's or dementia, which can cause folks to act or speak in some bizarre manner. For Christians to ascribe these conditions to demon possession is not only ignorant but also downright cruel. In His ministry, Jesus touched many who suffered in this way with His love, compassion, and healing.

One of the interesting things to me about those who in my opinion overemphasize miraculous physical healing is that I have never heard one of them claim healing for Alzheimer's disease. One of the things that compounds the difficulty is that the physical cause of Alzheimer's is coupled with the natural process of aging. It is a strong temptation to think that every older person who is forgetful or confused because of hearing or sight loss is showing symptoms of Alzheimer's, which of course is not the case.

An elderly man came to us, needing a place to live and since we had an extra apartment, we were happy to take him in. I'll call him Howard, which was not his real name. He was a fine looking individual about sixty years of age at that time, very warm and outgoing, someone who reminded you of your father or grandfather, and a professed, born-again Christian. He did not give any indication of a mental problem.

As time went by, we began to notice minor behavioral problems mostly associated with peculiar ideas. For example, our home was in the direct flight pattern for aircraft landing at a local airport. At about 10 PM each night the commuter plane from Boston would pass directly over our house and disappear over the hill toward the airport in Lebanon, NH. After being with us awhile, Howard began to indicate a particular interest in the plane and his ideas about it became more bizarre and unreasonable. It was not long before he was absolutely certain that the plane was loaded with IRS agents who were coming to investigate him.

It took me some time to realize that he was very serious about this and though we tried to reassure him that this was a ridiculous idea, his fixation on it only increased. Other fantasies began to reveal themselves in his life and we were becoming more and more aware that there was a serious mental problem. In fact, because his behavior was making him incompatible with the ministry we had, the question arose of how we should deal with it?

The climax came late one night. Howard had gone to Boston and we had reluctantly asked him to find other accommodations. It was about midnight and outside the temperature was near to zero, high piles of snow bordered the driveways, and there was a "pea soup" fog. I was preparing to go to bed when I heard a loud pounding on the door and someone shouting, "Does Howard live here?"

I hurried to the door and found a taxi driver standing there. He proceeded to tell me that he had driven Howard all the way from Boston, which was well over a hundred miles. When he had picked him up, he was dressed in an expensive winter suit and his appearance, as always, suggested wealth, so he had not considered asking him for advance payment. However, when he arrived in New Hampshire, Howard told him that he had no money to pay for the trip. The driver was quite shaken and wanted to use our phone to call his boss in Boston.

In the meantime, Howard was waiting in the cab. When the driver had completed his call, he went back outside only to return in a panic, shouting, "He took my cab! He took my cab!"

Picture this, a little old man, dressed in a business suit, who hadn't driven in years, taking a checkered cab, doing an impossible U-turn in the narrow driveway, speeding down the snow and ice covered hill in a fog so thick you could only see a few feet ahead.

There I was standing in my robe with a panicked cabbie in my living room, half crying, "There goes my job. He's going to wreck my cab!" I tried to console him with the fact that Howard couldn't get very far under those conditions. "He probably will only make it to the corner of the driveway and the snow bank will stop him," I said. In the meantime, the cabbie was calling the police. I could envision the message going out over the police radio. "There's a little old man driving a black and white taxicab with a light on the roof and we don't know where he went!" By this time I was dressed, and we were ready to take up the chase in our four-wheel drive truck.

Down the driveway we went, with no Howard in sight. Then out to the main road, and still no Howard! Which direction should we go? We didn't know, so we went up and down the road for several miles in both directions, and still there was no Howard in sight. All I could think to myself was, *That must have been some fantastic driving!*

Well, we could have gone miles out into the New Hampshire wilderness, looking, but we decided to go back home and wait for the police to find Howard, and shortly thereafter, they did. The cab was parked beside the highway with just a small scratch where he had pulled over and just brushed a guardrail. At 1:30 AM Howard was found walking down the state highway, still looking like a king. When the police offered him a ride and asked where he was going, he calmly told them, "To the supermarket, of course."

I still think highly of Howard, in fact, I believe we spiritually loved and accepted him and we provided temporary refuge. We later found that he had been in and out of hospitals and that he was supposed to be on certain controlling medications. Periodically, he rebelled against these and stopped taking them, whereupon his mental condition deteriorated. When it was controlled, he was as rational as anyone. Is there a lesson here for those pastors and parishioners who equate medication for specifically diagnosed disease with a lack of faith and, as a consequence, encourage these afflicted people to stop taking their medication? Is there a message for those who insist on calling all mental sickness demon possession?

There certainly is such a thing as "demon possession." In the accounts of Jesus' ministry there is ample evidence that He personally confronted spirit beings that had inhabited and controlled human lives. Luke 8:29 says, "For Jesus had commanded the evil spirit to come out of the man. Many times it had seized him, under guard. He had broken his chains and had been driven by the demon into solitary places."

I have heard personal testimony of missionaries who have

confronted "demon possession" on the foreign field. It was their observation that the individuals or groups involved usually performed super human feats or spoke in unusual voices. But if we are truly born again, it is not possible for Jesus to share His possession of us with demons. I, too, have had at least one experience with an individual that I felt was demon possessed. But before I relate the experience, I want to state that I do not believe that a truly born again child of God, saved by Jesus Christ, who has been sealed by the Holy Spirit, can be demon possessed. Jesus guaranteed that He personally would be the protecting shepherd of His people. John 10:25 promises, "My sheep listen to my voice; I know them and they follow me, no one can snatch them out of my hand."

In the Vermont State Prison where I served as Chaplain for six years, we had the criminally insane, because at that time the State of Vermont had no maximum-security accommodations at the state mental hospital. We had a psychologist, a little French man, with a very heavy accent, who visited the prison once a month to interview the mentally ill. Our office, which was at the far end of the visiting room, was directly across from the office used for interviews and counseling by the psychologist. The usual procedure was for an inmate to come into the visiting room, take a seat and wait to be called by the doctor. As he sat there, it was inevitable that the inmate would make all kinds of funny faces and gestures toward me, which I could clearly see through my glass door. These obviously indicated that the inmate thought that the psychologist was completely crazy! The men had some great jokes about the poor doctor who could not communicate with the staff, let alone the patients.

As a consequence of all this, the Catholic Chaplain and I found ourselves in the unenviable position of counseling the criminally insane inmates. It was a job that I did not enjoy, but one that enlightened me about insanity and its results. At that particular time, the legal definition for insanity in regard to crime was whether the accused defendant knew the difference between right and wrong at the time the crime was committed.

In my experience, I found that ordinary criminals could talk with me on a rational level about the wrong that had been done, whether they admitted doing it or not. The criminally insane, on the other hand without exception, were proud of what they had done and reveled in telling me, over and over again, all the gory details. Some of these were murders and some were sexual crimes. I hated to listen to those and told them so after the first time. Many of them told me that God had directed them to do what they did. Since then, I have always been careful about people who make such statements about being instructed directly by God.

In those years, Vermont still accepted sixteen and seventeen-year-olds in the maximum-security prison if the crime warranted it. On one occasion two young men, one sixteen and the other seventeen, were incarcerated, and one of them, the perpetrator of the crime, was judged criminally insane. It seems that an elderly gentleman had pulled into a rest stop in western Vermont at lunch time to have a sandwich and was sitting in his car, eating. These two young men casually walked up to the car, stuck a shotgun through the window and shot the man in the head for no apparent reason.

I'll never forget visiting this young man who was confined on death row, even though he had not been condemned to death. I had developed a theory that with these men that you always acted normally with them, both in your conversation and in your actions. You acted as casually as possible. I walked up to the cell and spoke directly to Tom (not his real name) and we struck up a conversation. I talked with him about the Lord and in response, he revealed a bit of his thinking. "We're like a guppy in a tank," he said. "There's a big eye looking in at us and controlling us."

I looked straight into his eyes and they were different and unusual. It appeared that while he was looking at me, he didn't see me at all. I cannot say for sure, but in my experience, I think that this young man reflected "demon possession," more than anyone else I have met in my years of ministry did. However, I feel more than ever that we must be extremely careful in our distinguishing and judging the difference between insanity caused by physiological problems and demon possession, which is totally different and whose direct source is Satan.

One of the features of the chaplaincy job was that we were always on 24-hour call. The warden at that time was a fine man, but emergency situations rattled him, and he got extremely nervous when they took place. I remember being called one night in the middle of winter. Two young inmates had slipped up to the roof of the furniture shop building and were threatening to burn it down. They had some flammable fluid. What they hoped to accomplish was beyond me, because they were on the roof of an old wooden building that was also located in the yard, surrounded by a thirty foot wall. The temperature was below zero. The warden was pacing back and forth, obviously nervous. At any rate, the local fire department solved the problem by soaking them down. They looked pretty pathetic, stripped down, with icicles hanging off their ears and noses as they were hustled back to their cells. Behavior is not always based upon reason. Often the problem of dealing with irrational behavior is dealing with those affected in a peripheral way, in this case, the Warden.

On another occasion, I was called personally by the Warden. A young man who went by the name of John Brown was threatening to burn himself. He had some lighter fluid in his cell. "Get right down here and see if you can talk to Brown. He's going to burn himself," the Warden said. The prison was only a short distance from our parsonage, so I was there in a matter of minutes. I knew "John" because we had talked on several occasions, and he claimed to be a Christian. Inside the cell, he presented a pathetic figure, disheveled, with a pained expression, holding a small bottle of fluid.

Coming up to the cell, I applied my theory of normalcy and calmness. "John," I asked, "what are you up to? Let's have a little talk about this!" I had found that no matter what the situation is, the best chance to diffuse it is to be casual and act as though you are continuing a discussion that you previously had.

"What's the problem?" I asked. John was already showing

signs of calming down. "They took away my TV," he said. I asked him why, and he said that the officers had been cursing at him and in response he had yelled at them. This turned out to be one occasion when he was telling the truth and after a discreet personal investigation, I found that there was one particular officer who singled out John as a target of his own personal anger and frustration. The situation was later corrected. A soft answer does turn away wrath in most cases.

Over the years, my idea concerning calm and normal responses to the mentally ill has been reinforced through further study and experience and, although it is not a guarantee, I strongly suggest it as a way to handle the mentally afflicted that come into your personal experience. No matter how strange or bizarre the behavior of the person, you must maintain a personal perception of calmness, normality, and reason! Sometimes you can broach the problem by asking a negative question, like, "John, you're not going to do something stupid, are you?"

As I see it, the third grouping of individuals who fall into the category of a "troubled mind" are those whose "altered behavior" is self-inflicted. Drug and alcohol abuse are the two biggest causes of this in today's society, but there is another more subtle yet just as devastating cause. It is the humanistic idea that we are not responsible before God for our actions. The first chapter of Romans deals with this subject extensively. It says that God gave man every opportunity to know Him and acknowledge Him. Romans 1:20 says, "For since the creation of the world, God's invisible qualities, His eternal power and divine nature have been clearly seen, being understood from what has been made, so that men are without excuse."

In turning away, two things happened. First, they rejected God and secondly, God gave them over to their own ways. The end result is devastating. Look at what happened! Romans 1:26-27 says, "Because of this, God gave them over to shameful lusts. Even their women exchanged natural relations for unnatural ones. In the same way the men also abandoned natural relations with women and were inflamed with lust for one another. Men committed indecent acts with other men and received in themselves the due penalty for their perversion."

This description of humanity with "God recognition" reads like tomorrow morning's newspaper. One cannot read Romans 1 without being struck by the fact that it is talking in specific terms about unnatural sexual habits. The key word here is "unnatural," men with men and women with women. One of the most troubling and disconcerting of today's challenges to us as Christians is to gain a proper perspective concerning "gays" and "lesbians." I personally do not believe that this is a "natural" lifestyle, as they would have us believe. During my prison ministry, I learned first hand that to inmates separated from a heterosexual relationship, homosexuality easily became a lifestyle. It was selfish, ugly, and brutal. The older, long-term inmates eyed the younger, good looking men arriving, and the result was man to man rapes, mind control, and ultimately horrible mental problems, and permanently ruined lives! In one case, it ultimately led to murder!

Have you ever wondered why the gay community must flaunt their lifestyle? Why do they need garish costumes, parades, and continual demonstrations? After all, they have gained political, and in some cases, social acceptance and no one is following them into the bedroom. Some time ago, in Provincetown, Massachusetts, the gay community held a parade complete with a lesbian motorcycle gang and large posters depicting oral and anal sex.

Is this kind of perverted, disgusting display of a totally unnatural, self-centered lifestyle going to invade the whole country as it has in San Francisco, New York, Cape Cod, and Key West? I'm afraid the answer is yes!

Our perspective as Christians must be to totally and completely reject homosexuality as repugnant to God and humanly abnormal. We must realize that the reason for the public display and outcry of gays is to gain social acceptability and to redefine the family unit. We must, in effect, find a way to hate the lifestyle while loving the life. The passage in Romans indicates that God gives them over to their lifestyle, together with its consequences.

It does not say that we should condemn them. Those who picket, carrying signs that say that God hates the homosexual are not only misled about God, but they are doing serious damage to the cause of Christ. We are not to hate them. Instead, if the opportunity presents itself, we should "pull them out of the fire."

As Christians, we must demonstrate to the gays, and potential gays, a marriage and friendship relationship with the opposite sex that is far superior to the cheap, degrading, counterfeit of homosexuality. Our example must be marked by love, caring, sensitivity, and most important, unselfishness. Thus, we can approach a repugnant movement with a positive message! The message of the cross and the resurrection is one of forgiven sins and newness of life. It can and does extend to the homosexual!

This discussion becomes especially important to those of us in our mature years, because we are best equipped to help those who seek a way out. As Christians, we have the answer. We know that Jesus came to "seek and to save that which was lost" and He did not come into the world to condemn the world but that "through Him the world might be saved."

We need not have been an addict or alcoholic to help those who are, but we do need the gifts we have previously mentioned of patience, love, and compassion, coupled with our knowledge of God's Word; and, we need to apply the years of valuable experience to each situation.

One of my duties as Chaplain at the Veterans' Hospital was to meet once a month with the Alcoholics Anonymous Group. AA has done a tremendous job working with alcohol addicted people and the church has no right to be critical of this excellent organization, since in most cases the church has done little to help. However, perhaps there is something we can add to the message of AA to make their program even more effective. Because of the religiously encompassing nature of the group, originally, the basic premise was that in order to overcome the addiction the individual must rely upon what was called "a higher power." The addicts, in other words, must admit that they cannot do it in their own strength.

In more recent times, the words used in the handbook have been changed from "higher power" to "God," which is surely a step in the right direction. My observation to the group was about that very thing. I felt that the idea of a non-personal "higher power" left me cold and that Christianity could add a more complete dimension. Jesus Christ came for the very purpose of being a Savior, Lord, and personal friend to each individual. I found the group to be very receptive.

As we come to the "other side of life," we cannot abdicate our responsibility to the world around us. We can continue, throughout all the years of our lives, touching others for God. Jude 21-23 says, "Be merciful to those who doubt; snatch others from the fire and save them; to others show mercy, mixed with fear, hating even the clothing stained by corrupt flesh."

Questions for individual or group use may be found in the Appendix, which begins on Page 141.

11

SKYHOOKS, SNIPES, AND LEFT-HANDED MONKEY WRENCHES

During World War II, I was a teenager. In the summer, we were enlisted to work in War plants. At 60 cents an hour, working for the Dupont Company seemed like a great opportunity to me, so I went to work at my first real job.

Now, I knew about the "hazing" that occurs in college, but I was pretty naïve about what happened in factories. So, on one of my first days at work, my boss said to me, "I want you to go down to the finishing department and get me a sky hook."

Down the long aisle I went, through every department with their machines churning away and people busily working – a new world to me – in search of a "sky hook."

Imagine my surprise when I finally arrived at the end of the building and asked the mechanics for a sky hook. From their smiles and comments, it only took a second for me to realize the truth that I had been taken! The "skyhooks" on helicopters today had not yet been invented. As I remember it, though, together with the feeling of complete stupidity, there was a certain sense of achievement because when I sheepishly returned to my department, I really belonged to the crew for the first time.

That feeling increased not long thereafter, when my boss sent me off to find a "left-handed monkey wrench." I was young, eager to please, and not mechanically inclined, so I did what I was told, only to see the smiles and hear the laughter of the crew, again.

Many of us have gone out into the world looking for something that didn't exist. One of those things, unfortunately, is something that was of utmost concern to Jesus – something for which He earnestly prayed – that there would be unity in the Body of Christ.

After sixty years in the Lord's work, I can honestly say that, despite all the rhetoric, there is now no more unity in the church (in a universal sense) than there ever was. In spite of all the dangers, enemies, and challenges to the Christian faith, there is simply no doubt that believers are not "one in the Spirit." I have wrestled with this problem. I have tried to make a difference, but I must admit that after all this time, little or no progress has been made. In fact, things may be worse now than when I first entered the ministry more than sixty years ago.

For the church, the real world in which we live is full of real challenges. Nothing is as simple as it appears to be, especially when the picture is painted by media personalities who seem driven not by Christ's power, but by their own desire for fame or fortune. Labels are part of the problem. Some call themselves "fundamentalists," "evangelical," "spirit-filled," "conservative," and the like. Yet the only real issue is which of these are truly followers of Jesus.

Regardless how important the spokespersons may attach to these labels, I have absolutely no doubt that these labels matter not in the least to God, who might ask every person who labels himself or herself in any way, "Why must you call yourself anything other than Christian? After all, it was good enough for the early church."

The net effect of every label that believers apply to themselves is that the label not only separates that person from the rest of Christ's body, but it PUT'S DOWN (whether overtly or subtly) other Christians who may not share the same convictions in areas that seem irrelevant when you consider the bigger picture – specifically, that the world is full of people who neither know Jesus nor know what He taught. If the primary way they are to learn is through us, then we have to be saying the same thing.

I could tell you a hundred stories, maybe a thousand, about how true seekers of the truth have been driven away from the One who is the way, the truth, and the life, as a result of things that were added to the simple gospel by those whose fellowship they sought. For example, some think you have to worship in a certain way, without instruments (this is just one of many additions), or with speaking of tongues, or being baptized in a certain way, or adhering to a certain man's doctrines (for example, Calvin or Luther), or even using only certain translations of the Bible – most notably the King James Version, which they love to call the "authorized" version, though its authorization was by a king, not the King). I could go on and on. Baptists, Lutherans, Pentecostals – everybody seems to have "their thing," when the only question important to God is whether or not they ARE the real thing – that is followers of Jesus, committed to loving the Lord their God with all their hearts, souls, mind, and strength … and their neighbors as themselves.

Let's just consider the label "fundamentalists." Some people love to call themselves Christian fundamentalists, though they can't seem to see how this links them with other fundamentalists, worldwide, including Islamic fundamentalists. If I say that I am a Christian fundamentalist, and I take pride in that label I have attached to myself, on the one hand the implication is that I believe in the fundamentals of the Christian faith. At the same time, though, my label implies that other Christians do not believe in the fundamentals of the Christian faith, which is certainly not true. If I refer to my church as a "spirit-filled" church, am I not implying that other Christian churches are not spirit-filled?

As we reach our senior years, most of us realize how trivial (and how detrimental) majoring in these minor issues can be to the mission we've been given by Christ. However, finding a church family that also realizes this is more difficult than it ought to be.

At the retreat center we founded in New Hampshire, everyone pitches in to do the physical work. On one occasion, though I was the president, I was in the kitchen washing dishes (an activity that I actually enjoyed). One of the ministers who was there on a retreat approached me and asked me if I spoke in tongues. I answered him as I have always answered this question, "Although I am open to anything that God wants for me, I have not spoken in tongues."

"Do you know that our church was the first to speak in tongues, and we are the only ones who are genuine?" he asked.

My first thought was that I wished he had the gift of "helps," as

I could really use some help cleaning up after him and his group. But what I said was, "I understand that others before you have spoken in tongues, most notably the early believers on the Day of Pentecost. I'm also aware that many other Pentecostal or Charismatic churches employ this gift in their worship. So ... I think you would do well to revisit your claims to be first or best, since Jesus said the first shall be last and the last, first."

Pride always comes before a fall. The pride and superficiality, and downright biblical and theological ignorance that spawns them, must be purged from the Body of Christ today if we are ever to truly fulfill Christ's prayer, with the result that the world will know we are one, by our love. This is the only way that outside observers will care to know more about Him.

I call all senior Christians to make a genuine effort to love and respect our brothers and sisters in Christ. We have experience; we have perspective; we have wisdom – all of which the younger generation can benefit from.

Meanwhile, we must stop sending those behind us out searching for something that does not exist. When I worked with young people, we had a lot of fun during our periodic "snipe" hunts. Yes, there is a bird called a "snipe." But the kind of snipe I'm talking about exists only in one's most vivid imagination, which is why young people are most intrigued by the endeavor. Many a youth leader has given his subjects a gunny sack, a flashlight, a stick, and a whistle, and sent them out into the dark forest to hunt the elusive snipe. "If you crawl on the ground," the leader suggests, "and hold the gunny sack open, and beat the ground with a stick, and blow your whistle, then into your trap the snipe will run. When this happens, you must quickly close the sack and head back to the rendezvous place, being careful that the snipe does not escape."

Believe it or not, in my youth I was one of those who came back with scratches, mosquito bites, and an empty sack, still believing that there were snipes out in those woods, just waiting to be captured. Today's kids might be smarter than that. With all the technological stuff at their disposal, including their cell phones, they can check out the authenticity of a "snipe hunt," or the authenticity of someone's claim regarding what it means to follow Jesus.

When we talk to young people today about Christ, we need to be honest with them. We don't want to send them out looking for a skyhook, a snipe, or even a left-handed monkey wrench. We want them to be seeking the real thing, the real Person who can give their life meaning, direction, and fulfillment, perhaps even for the next sixty years, as has happened for me.

I made a decision some time ago that whenever I had an opportunity to speak to young people, I would make the Christian life sound as hard as possible. I would tell them the truth – like Jesus told His potential disciples to take up their crosses and follow Him. I would tell them that peer pressures would be fierce. They might have to stand alone in their school or on their athletic team. They might be forsaken by friends and lose their popularity, should they decide to stand up for Jesus.

Not too long ago, I spoke to a group of Junior High students, about seventeen in number. I used Scripture to describe the cost of living for Christ. At the end, I gave an invitation to accept Christ as their Savior, and fourteen responded positively.

The world is real. The enemies are real. But Jesus is REALITY. But in order to follow Him, their faith must be real enough to find blessedness in this unique way: "Blessed are you when people insult you, persecute you, and falsely say all kinds of evil against you, because of Me."

Questions for individual or group use may be found in the Appendix, which begins on Page 141.

CONCLUSION:

FROM PERCEPTION TO REALITY - OUR JOURNEY THROUGH LIFE

"When I was a child, I talked like a child, I thought like a child, I reasoned like a child. When I became a man, I put childish things behind me" (1 Corinthians 13:11).

Great Grandma Brooks could sit for hours, telling me fascinating stories about her childhood during the Civil War. Yet, she had difficulty remembering events that had happened just a few hours before.

We all have a "memory bank," and events and experiences from the past are stored up there in the safe deposit box of the mind. Perhaps you, like me, have found it more difficult to access these memories as you grow older.

There are words we can't remember, faces we can't quite place, and appointments that we forget. Yet, this information is vitally important to us as we try to understand our life now and put it into its proper perspective. That is because our life today consists of the "input" of all the experiences since our birth. Our life "essence" is composed of "perception," "imagination," and "reality," together with heredity and environment as a base.

Before we take one last look in the mirror, let me illustrate this concept. "Perception" can be defined as "awareness or consciousness of events, people, or things as they relate to us." Perceptions played a critical role in our childhood development when the school of trial and error was a constant companion and a hard teacher. Yet, I am convinced that, as children, we had little, if any, real understanding of what was really happening to us.

Before the advent of television there was a certain "innocence" of childhood that is missing today. The current media concept of the adolescent is that of a self-confident, egotistical, "know it all" individual whose sophisticated knowledge includes everything from sex to Star Wars.

The idea of childhood "omniscience" is reinforced because many children now know how to use computers while their parents do not. But a child is still a child! A computer is not "experiential" in nature; it is simply a machine programmed by a human mind. When society permits and even encourages the "computer" information of children and young people to replace knowledge and wisdom obtained by valuable experience, there is often a short circuit, the sparks fly, the fire starts, and all too often there is disaster!

This brings us to the idea of what role "perceptions" played in the formation of our lives. I believe that most of our perceptions as children came from our relationships with adults. One of the saddest trends of our time is the increasing incidence of abuse and abandonment of children. This produces a vicious cycle in which parents produce offspring who often follow in their harmful and destructive lifestyles, for example, addicts producing addicts, abusers producing abusers, and on and on. This is a cycle that is almost impossible to interrupt and reverse. Only the "grace of God" and re-creation by the Holy Spirit can intervene! As 2 Corinthians 5:17 says, "If any man is in Christ, he is a new creation, old things pass away and all things become new."

We have a neighbor - we'll call him Bill - who periodically screams in frustration at this family. Though he claims to be a devoted Christian, he shouts and screams at his wife and small children. He seems oblivious to his neighbors and to the effect upon the children. It is very confusing to hear the harshness of anger rising above the sweet sound of Sandi Patti coming from his stereo. How do you think these children will respond to frustration when they grow up? Aside from that, how many of his neighbors do you think will be attracted to his Christ or to his church?

Many of us were particularly blessed, as children, with strong family ties and an abundance of good role models. My mother and dad gave me a solid "life foundation" upon which to build. I also had an assortment of outstanding examples, including teachers, pastors, family members, and friends. In addition, I had numerous "aunts and uncles," most of whom were not really blood relations. It seemed to me that every older man was an "uncle" and every older woman was an "aunt." These people, though not the closest to me, made a tremendous contribution to the building of my life, even though, at the time, I was not aware of it.

Uncle Fred owned a dairy and I always liked to visit him at his home in the country. He could make funny faces by taking out his false teeth, putting his fingers in his mouth, and puffing out his cheeks. Then, there was that long window couch in his house. Somehow, he and I would always find some bright, shiny coins under those cushions. He enjoyed making children happy. Uncle Fred demonstrated to me a special kind of humor and fun that later put a twinkle in my eyes and became a part of my life.

Uncle Charlie was a little different. He was actually a second cousin and also my high school biology teacher. I entered high school during World War II, when many young men could only see a military career ahead of them, and thus developed an "I don't care" attitude about studies. This idea was reinforced by the "body count" of service men returning from the battlefields in coffins. I was among those who developed an antipathy toward education and began to drift my way through high school - until "Uncle Charlie" entered the picture. "Biebel, bat your head on that table and get some brains in it," he would say. It may have been a bit crude, but after some complaining on my part, the message finally got through. If I wanted to go to college, I had to study. These people and many others imparted the perceptions that helped me, in the end, to form my life "strategy." As these perceptions were incorporated into my behavior, they became, in turn, the very essence of my life and shaped the person I am today.

The perceptions that we communicate to others are vitally important. As Christians, on the "other side of life," we are offered a golden opportunity to demonstrate to those coming after us the genuine love and caring of Jesus Christ. We must never discourage young people from searching for the truth. Rather, it is our responsibility to channel their God-given desire to learn and know toward the spiritual side of life, toward the "life giver."

We must reveal to them by our example that the Christian faith is both "close ended" and "open-ended." That we present this concept to non-Christians is especially important because of the current superficial, anti-intellectual approach taken by some well-known evangelists and preachers. The Christian faith and the Bible, itself, are packed with invitations to test its promises and conclusions concerning life.

Until Jesus came, we had only "perceptions" of what God was like. The incarnation of God's only begotten Son changed all that. "The Word became flesh and lived among us and we beheld His glory, the only begotten of the Father, full of grace and truth."

Childhood was a time of perceiving and adapting. Late adolescence and young adulthood became a period of "imagination." We could dream fantastic dreams, plan great events, perform unbelievable feats, all in our mind. When these fantasies became a part of behavior, they became experiments. Sometimes these were successful, and at other times they ended in disaster.

I was involved in one such incident. I call it "Snap, Crackle, Pop!" It happened shortly after we discovered potassium permanganate. One of the exciting things we learned in chemistry lab was that small crystals of potassium permanganate, when crushed, produce miniature explosions. In the fantasy world of high school social life, this discovery opened the door to many wonderful options. The one that I chose, together with a friend, was to spread some of these crystals on the locker room floor, after everyone else had gone upstairs to the gym.

Before I tell you what happened, I should note here that during this phase of imagination, we very seldom considered the possible consequences.

At any rate, imagine our excitement, when, during the gym class, we began to hear loud noises echoing up the stairs from the locker room - Snap, Crackle, and Pop! This was a grand moment, the experiment was working! That was until the school principal, Mr. Roth, appeared in the doorway with a decided frown on his face and demanded to know who had planted the "booby trap." My friend and I hadn't counted on the fact that each little explosion left a beautiful purple stain. In this case, Principal Roth stood there displaying two unusually decorated purple shoes. The result for us was long hours of detention, a lesson earned and well learned.

I have a suspicion that many others now on "the other side of life" once tried an experiment like that in their youth, too.

Young adulthood didn't alter the situation very much, as we continued to experiment. The difference with today's young men and women is in the kind of experiments they try. Ours often had a humorous, sometimes even mischievous ending! Today, they often end in disability or even death. Alcohol, drugs, and casual sex are experiments in behavior that are like bombs waiting to go off, poisons waiting to kill.

The young man, Solomon, decided to satisfy his curiosity by experimenting with every possible lifestyle, and he had the resources to do it! Because of his great wealth, he was able to bring all the common ingredients to himself such as wine, women, and song. He poured all his energy into this search for happiness. He gathered to himself servants, material excesses, food, drink, orchestras, and everything that expressed the later Epicurean philosophy of "Eat, drink and be merry, for tomorrow we die."

As he proceeded through his experiment, Solomon found that each new diversion produced within him the same conclusion, that "all is vanity and vexation of spirit." It was a demeaning, frustrating, even life-threatening conclusion to the experiment and to his imaginations.

Not all imaginations, though, end in disaster. Some result in amazing discoveries and inventions. Then there are those that end with a laugh! In college, I was one of five roommates in a large dorm room. This room was reminiscent of an ancient prison, bare except for an army cot, a small desk, and a bureau for each student. The ceiling was so high that we had a standing joke about planes flying through on their way to the local airport. Trying to live and study in that environment was no joke! It was tough!

We had one particular roommate named Dave, who was a good fellow at heart, but because of his loud and unruly habits, he got on our collective nerves. For example, when he went out in the evening and returned late, he tended to forget that the rest of us were already in bed. He had gigantic feet and would come clomping up the stairs, burst into the room, slamming the door behind him, and then proceed directly to the bathroom. There he seemed to delight in flushing the toilet five or six times, spitting and gargling with particularly disgusting sounds. Finally, one night, when he was out, we had a council of "war" and decided to "fix" him when he returned.

With great ingenuity we arranged a pail of water over the door in such a way that when he opened the door, the bucket would tip and the water would find its target on Dave's head. This we did, and then we waited with great anticipation. We could hardly contain ourselves when finally we heard footsteps coming up the stairs and stopping just outside the door - perfect! The moment was here, the door began to open, the bucket tipped, and the water came down with a huge splash! After a moment, the light came on and there in the doorway, dripping with water from head to toe stood, not Dave, but the Dean!

After an appropriate period of silence, the Dean, being a man of great wisdom spoke calmly, "Men, I suggest that you clean up this mess and get some sleep, because you definitely will need it." The outcome of our great imagination and experiment resulted in many long hours of "KP" duty in the college dining room.

Through the early phases of our life we are encouraged by the Word of God to search, to investigate, even to test His promises. This is the "open-ended" part of our spiritual lives:

"O taste and see that the Lord is good."

"Ask and it shall be given you, seek and you shall find."

"Knock and it shall be opened to you."

"You shall seek Me and find Me when you search for Me with all your heart."

The Bible, more than any other book, encourages a continuance of seeking and searching. The reason is simple. God is not afraid of any truth we may discover. At the same time, the fundamental truths of the Bible, once studied, understood, and accepted, become "close ended" to the Christian. That's faith, and it is faith in the final analysis that leads to reality!

To me, there are two kinds of reality. The first is philosophical or spiritual in nature. It is "what I believe," the intellectual faith commitment that I have made. It consists of all those things I believe about God, the Bible, the world around me, and my own life. Without this side of reality, I would literally be "lost," having no foundation for my life now and no hope for the future. As I see it, this "reality" for me is founded in one basic fact of history, the resurrection of Jesus Christ!

I was long confused as to why the Apostle Paul said in 1 Corinthians that if Jesus is not raised from the dead, we as Christians would be "of all people, the most miserable." I would think that even if Christ were not alive today, I would still be completely happy with my Christian commitment and lifestyle.

Then I realized that Paul was really talking about what it would mean for a person to be living a whole life committed to a belief that was false - a delusion! That truly would be pathetic. So, I am back again to the fact that I DO BELIEVE - my faith is real! It is consistent with everything I have read, learned, studied, or experienced. It is the very "substance" of my life.

My heart goes out to those who have turned the corner of life and still do not possess a basic faith. I can only love them and be caring and sharing in my relationships, hoping and praying that they may see a bit of Christ living in me and seek Him for themselves.

There is another kind of "reality," which concerns my daily life; in other words, what I do and how I act. James reminded us in the first chapter of his letter that we are to be "doers of the

Word, not just hearers." Let me share with you what "reality" in daily living means to me, now that I am over eighty years of age:

REALITY - is how I handle the first hour of the morning when I wake up feeling weak, tired, and hurting.

REALITY - is the kind of sensitivity I have toward my wife, my family, and friends in their needs, hopes, and aspirations.

REALITY - is how I overcome the depressions and fears associated with growing older, and eroding health.

REALITY - is the kind of person I am under stress and in the midst of frustration.

REALITY - is how much I am willing to sacrifice to help someone in need.

REALITY - is what I do with my money and material possessions.

REALITY - is how I handle temptation when it is staring me in the face.

REALITY - is how I respond to emergencies, sudden loss and tragedies.

Jesus' human life was relatively short, about thirty years. Packed into that life was so much meaning, so much reality! Besides coming to be our Savior, Jesus came to teach us how to live. Did you ever stop to think that the recorded events, experiences, and teaching of Jesus recorded in the Bible cover only a fraction of those thirty years? What about the rest? The answer is that He, too, lived a "daily life." The Word became flesh and "lived" among us. That is the reason He is able to be with us and share the challenges that often bring us down.

Hebrews 4:15-16 says, "For we do not have a great high priest who cannot be touched with the feelings of our weaknesses; but One who was tempted in all points, just as we are, yet without sin. Let us therefore come boldly to His throne of grace, that we may obtain mercy and find grace to help in time of need" (Paraphrased).

CONCLUSION

Well, here we are back at the mirror again! As I take another look, I notice several unique things about the mirror. It is no longer just a reflection of my appearance. In fact, it is no longer just a mirror! I see other images. It is more like a beautiful mural. I see myself walking down a path, but not alone. There is another Person walking with me. Ahead in the distance, there are mountains and valleys and the path takes me toward them. Along the way there are people and places. I can't see the end of the path, but I know where it is leading. There are others on the path with me, those I know and love. I am deeply moved as I gaze, and suddenly I am aware - this is not just a mural either, but a "plan." To think that I can be part of it!

THE MIRROR OF MY LIFE

In the chambers of my imagery, I saw myself,
Young and full of hope!
Later, I saw myself, indulged in life,
So busy - so many plans.
Then I saw another person - real!
And I knew that time was fleeing away.
Then I saw the Lord, caring and loving,
I knew He still had a plan for me.
Then I understood the really important
things in life
These were already mine! And so ...
I no longer needed to dream a dream of life -
Because God's kind of life belongs to me!

The Lord is my Shepherd
He satisfies all my needs
He teaches me to appreciate the blessings of life
He lifts up my spirit
He walks before me and shows me the right path
Even when danger or death are near, I need not be afraid
His Holy Spirit and His Word comfort me
He nourishes me with courage when
enemies are all around
His Spirit touches me so that I can help others
All my days will be filled with His blessings
And I will live with Him forever
(My paraphrase of the twenty-third Psalm)

THERE IS NO BETTER PLAN!

Questions for individual or group use may be found in the Appendix, which begins on the following page.

APPENDIX

QUESTIONS FOR PERSONAL REFLECTION AND/OR GROUP DISCUSSION

Note: You may prefer to keep your answers to the following questions in a separate notebook or journal. Most likely, you will wish to keep private some of your responses; some you may choose to share with others. The main thing is to respond as honestly as possible, since, in the end, personal growth is between yourself and the Lord, who desires truth in your inner being, so that He can help you grow in wisdom (Psalm 51: 5-6).

Chapter 1: Going South in the Northbound Lane

1. When you look in the "mirror," do you see someone who is: a) primarily struggling for survival; b) still experiencing expansion of your horizons; or c) a little of both? Which "person" do you like better?

2. If you believe that God still has a plan for you, try to express your understanding of that plan in a sentence or two.

3. List some of the ways you hope to fulfill God's plan for you, and what you hope will be the results.

4. In general, do you view your age as an asset or an excuse? Give an example of how this expresses itself, practically, in your attitudes or actions.

5. What Scriptures help you prepare for and face the inevitable adversity that comes with aging?

Chapter 2: A Bridge Over Troubled Waters

1. If you had all the power and opportunity necessary to

function as a "living bridge" for the younger generations across an accelerating span of social and political change, what would this "look like" in action? What would you try to accomplish? Would your primary focus be positive and constructive or negative and critical? With whom would you wish to share your knowledge and wisdom? Note: In a group setting, try "role playing" your first attempt to provide a member of the "now" generation with a longer-term view of things (see pages 32-33 for some ideas to discuss, or make up your own). Have two volunteers role play this discussion. One of them is nineteen, a freshman in college studying nothing in particular; the other a sixty-six-year-old veteran or retired history professor. After three minutes of discussion, with the group taking notes, reverse roles and go for three more minutes. Then have the group discuss how best to try to bridge any gaps that may exist.

2. In your own experience, how easy or difficult has it been to exchange the role of being a person in authority for that of an advisor and counselor? What Scriptures, biblical examples, or biblical principles guided you in this process?

3. How might praying the prayer on page 38 be helpful to those having trouble keeping their bearings as they make such transitions?

4. What role might a sense of humor play in opening doors of communication or countering frustrations when seeking to act as a "bridge over troubled waters"?

Chapter 3: If the Ship Leaks, Is It Sinking?

1. Philippians 4:4-7 describes the secret of having peace versus anxiety in your hearts and minds. Read this passage in your favorite translation. In a group setting have someone read it aloud. Or use the following, my personal paraphrase, which can be found in my book, *We've Got Mail* (page 58):

Now, here is some important advice. You need to be happy and there's nothing wrong in showing it. And in this day of excess, you can show your faith to the lost by your self-control. Knowing that Jesus is with you will remind you to do this. You need a sense of release when it comes to sharing your problems and needs with God. Don't hold anything back. The result will be that God provides you with a special kind of peace that you have never before experienced. He will have complete control of your emotions and minds and that will give you a deep sense of security.

There are some great things to think about, even though the world around us is so evil. Things that are true and good, lovely and honest, just and pure - these are the kind of thoughts that deserve your focus. Dwelling on these thoughts will produce mental and spiritual health and overall well-being in your life.

What specific steps can we take to calm our anxieties? List everything that comes to mind. In a group setting, list these steps so all can see and copy the list.

2. If retaining one's best possible health is a prerequisite to loving the Lord with our whole strength, would that imply that trying to live in a healthy way is a spiritual matter as well as a physical matter? What Scriptures or biblical principles come to mind in relation to living healthily?

3. Do you think that the church in general has had a blind spot in relation to healthy living? If so, what can be done or is being done to align the church's view on this with that of God?

4. How can we best practice the kind of godly tolerance and respect that is expressed in Romans 14:2-3 when we see someone who is obviously ignoring his or her health or when we witness something in a church setting (such as 2,000 Calorie desserts or greasy fast food at a church supper)?

5. Do you agree with Percy Crawford's perspective (page 48) that, as Christ's ambassadors, we should strive to be as attractive as possible as part of our witness to unbelievers? If so, how does this relate to our weight, how we conduct ourselves in public, how we drive, the way we dress, or even to such things as the use of "Grecian Formula," "Rogaine," plastic surgery, cosmetics? Is there a line that should not be crossed? If you believe so, what is your biblical basis for that belief?

Chapter 4: Don't Throw That Club!

1. One component of mental health is that a person needs to have at least one good friend. How would you describe the best friend you have ever had? Make a list of all the words that come to mind, and share them, if meeting with a group.

2. Recall how you met that person and how the friendship developed over time. Looking back, what was the key component (or what were the key components) that made the difference between just being acquaintances and becoming best friends? For example, some would list: we worked together toward a common goal; or, we regularly shared a common recreational interest, or a hobby. Share your list with others, and come up with ten or more components that contribute to long-lasting, deep friendships.

3. The friendship of David and Jonathan is one of the Bible's most moving accounts. Read 1 Samuel 18:1-4; 20:1-42 and list all the words that describe the emotion and commitment involved in this godly friendship. What hinders the such intensity in friendships today? What opportunities does

modern life afford through which friendships can be sustained over time, even at long distances?

Chapter 5: Bank Accounts, IOUs, and Bouncing Checks

1. If you have not made adequate provision for your senior years, what can you do now about that?

2. Are you handling your finances wisely? If so, what are the components of your current financial management? If these are shared in a group setting, make a list of the ten most common principles mentioned.

3. Do you make provision in your budget (assuming you have a budget) for the needs of God's work? What Scriptures or biblical principles do you feel apply, both specifically and broadly to your approach to giving? For example, do you believe your local church and/or denomination should be the primary recipient of your tithes and offerings? Or do you view the work of God in a broader sense, including parachurch organizations or even non-religious charities that are focused on helping the poor and needy? Have you made plans to include certain favorite charities or organizations in the disbursement of your assets after your death? If so, what guidelines or guidance did you find most useful in making such decisions?

4. In 2 Corinthians 9:6-11, Paul outlines certain important elements of faithful giving. See how many of these you can identify, and share your answers:

> Now this I say, he who sows sparingly will also
> reap sparingly, and he who sows bountifully will
> also reap bountifully. Each one must do just as he
> has purposed in his heart, not grudgingly or
> under compulsion, for God loves a cheerful giver.
> And God is able to make all grace abound to you,

so that always having all sufficiency in everything, you may have an abundance for every good deed; as it is written,

> "HE SCATTERED ABROAD, HE GAVE TO THE POOR, HIS RIGHTEOUSNESS ENDURES FOREVER."

Now He who supplies seed to the sower and bread for food will supply and multiply your seed for sowing and increase the harvest of your righteousness; you will be enriched in everything for all liberality, which through us is producing thanksgiving to God (NASB).

Chapter 6: Bells, Buzzers, and Whistles

1. What are your own keys to living a life of serenity in spite of today's social chaos?

2. How do you deal with unacceptable things that are portrayed in the media?

3. Review Psalm 31, where the psalmist describes many feelings that can go with aging, but finds solace and peace in knowing his "times" are in the Lord's hands. How does this confidence rooted in faith affect you in relation to the bells, buzzers, and whistles of life?

Chapter 7: Doing Business in Great Waters – Dealing with Current Events

1. To what degree do you think that believers should become political activists? Do you have any Scriptures or biblical principles that guide your opinion on this matter?

2. Revisionism is a key point of this chapter and a key

plague in our world today, affecting so many areas including constitutional law, criminal law and justice, politics, finances, business and business practices, education (especially the teaching of history), theology and biblical studies, and the practice of religion. It seems that wherever you look, not just the rules have changed, but the facts have been amended to suit the interests of the amender. What examples have you noticed of this phenomenon, and what do you think believers should do when they encounter it in:

__law
__politics
__business
__education
__theology and biblical studies
__religious practices
__the reporting of one's golf score (joke)

3. Review Jesus' statement about being the salt of the earth (Matthew 5:13-16) in light of my thoughts about this (pages 74-75). What principles guide you in finding a faithful balance of belief and action in this arena?

Chapter 8: Thunder and Lightning

1. Are you afraid of lightning; of storms such as hurricanes or tornadoes; of other natural disasters such as floods or earthquakes or wildfires Tsunamis or volcano eruptions - or even just the possibility of these? List words that come into your mind when you think of each of the above possibilities.

2. Name your greatest fear, and where it seems to have originated. How long has this fear dogged you, and what effects has it had on your personal and social life?

3. Search the Scriptures for what is said there about fear and God's attitudes and actions in relation to our fears (don't forget to search for the word "afraid," as well as "fear." Make a

list of all the verses you can find, and share them in a group setting. What insights do you gain by reviewing these, including what seems to be God's attitude toward our fears? Does He condemn us for harboring fear from time to time? What does He offer most often as an antidote to our fears? Which verses minister most to you today?

4. Have you ever had what seemed to have been a divine intervention that saved you from serious injury or death? Describe what happened, and then stop and thank the Lord in prayer that He cared enough to sent a ministering spirit to you at just the right time (see Hebrews 1:14).

Chapter 9: Unitarians, Fire, and Personal Integrity

1. Give an example from your own experience or observation where spokespersons who thought they were "the good guys" made judgments about "the bad guys" in terms of why they deserved bad things to happen to them. (For example, some well-known Christian media types have embarrassed themselves and perhaps confused the gospel message for many by making condemnatory statements about why bad things happened to Haiti, for example, or why bad things happened to the pornography producing area in California (both earthquakes). How does this compare to what Jesus taught in: Luke 13:4, the message of John 9:1-4, or the meaning of Matthew 5:43-48?

2. Write out your own definition of personal integrity. From your own experience or observation, give an example of how integrity expresses itself in real life.

3. If you think that "spiritual integrity" differs from personal integrity in a generic sense, specify what the difference(s) may be. Give an example here, also.

4. Have you had the personal experience of having con-

demned someone only to realize, later, that as a follower of Jesus and in relation to His teachings regarding judging, you had missed the mark? (see Luke 6:37-42)

5. Extra credit: Why do you think that some modern believers think themselves superior enough to pass judgment on anyone at all?

Chapter 10: The Other Side of the Other Side of Life

1. How do you ordinarily relate to the mentally disabled or afflicted (including those with depression, bipolar disorder, schizophrenia, epilepsy - which is a disease with physical causes, of course - retardation, and so forth) in your circle of acquaintances? Do you:

__try to help them as best you can
__try to avoid them as much as possible
__thank the Lord you are not like them
__wonder what they did to deserve such a state
__try to help them gain a sense of meaning and dignity

2. How do you view and relate to those who are struggling with addictions (usually construed as self-imposed) such as addiction to drugs, alcohol, gambling, sex, or pornography - to name a few so-called "addictions"? Do you:

__leave them to their own punishments for their choices
__try to help them by loving and encouraging them
__turn them in to the appropriate authorities
__turn my back on them
__feel happy and self-justified that I am not like them
__try to get them the help they need
__other: _____

3. If you know someone addicted to any of these things, what do you think Jesus would say to him or her?

Chapter 11: Skyhooks, Snipes, and Left-handed Monkey Wrenches

1. If you've ever had someone play a trick on you like those that were played on me - write it down, and laugh. For the most part, people take themselves too seriously, so here's a way to laugh at yourself and to be grateful for those who gave you the chance to do so.

2. Now, on to more serious stuff - unity in the church. Why do you think there is so much disunity, competition, judgmental attitudes, and so forth, in the church as we know it today?

3. How do you feel about my wish that we could forego labels like fundamental, evangelical, spirit-filled, conservative, and so forth and just get back to being followers of Jesus?

4. My challenge here is: "I call all senior Christians to make a genuine effort to love and respect our brothers and sisters in Christ. We have experience; we have perspective; we have wisdom - all of which the younger generation can benefit from. Do you agree? Disagree? Not care?

5. But the key to this chapter is what we communicate to those coming behind. We must not encourage them to search for something that does not exist. No skyhooks, snipes, or left-handed monkey wrenches - just reality, whose name is Jesus. How can we help them get to know Him, without hype, denominationalism, or anything other than truth? See if you can come up with even one way, and share this with your group. May your group become a movement, and your movement the re-revealing of the truth that is in Him, alone.

Conclusion: From Perception to Reality – Our Journey Through Life

1. If our "golden" opportunity in our "golden" years is to demonstrate to those coming after us the genuine love and caring of Jesus Christ, where do you think the best opportunities for doing this might occur - in a secular setting or in the setting of the church?

2. If there are two kinds of "realty - philosophical/spiritual reality and the reality of our daily lives - how do we best bring these into a type of co-existence that produces good results? Sometimes they seem to be in conflict; other times not. How do you approach this conundrum?

3. On page 138, I list eight "realities" of living, a self-examination routine that helps me stay focused and on track. If these make sense to you, rank them 1-8 from easiest to most difficult to fulfill, #1 being the most difficult:

__how I respond to emergencies, sudden loss, and tragedies

__how I handle the first hour of the morning when I wake up feeling weak, tired, and hurting

__how I overcome the depressions and fears associated with growing older, including eroding health

__ my level of sensitivity toward my spouse, family, and friends and their needs, hopes, and aspirations

__what kind of person I am under stress or when experiencing frustration

__how much I am willing to sacrifice to help someone in need

__what I do with my money and material possessions, in general

__how I handle temptation when it is staring me in the face

Resources from Healthy Life Press

Unless otherwise noted on the site itself, shipping is free for all products purchased through www.healthylifepress.com.

New Releases – Fall 2014

Mommy, What's 'Died' Mean? - How the Butterfly Story Helped Little Dave Understand His Grandpa's Death, by Linda Swain Gill; Illustrated by David Lee Bass (a.k.a. "Little Dave") – Designed to assist Christian parents and other adults who love and care about children to talk with them about the difficult subject of death, the story traces a small child's experience following his grandpa's and shows how his mother sensitively answered his questions about death by using simple examples derived from the birth of a butterfly. Little Dave's story is colorfully illustrated and designed for a child and parent or trusted adult to read together. The story has been created especially for children from pre-kindergarten through 4th grade. Discussion questions are included for each story page to help determine how much the child understands. A simple imitation game is also included to help involve the child in the story. Several pages at the end of the book contain suggestions about how to discuss death and dying with children of various ages. (**Full-color printed book:** $14.99; PDF eBook: $9.99; both together: $19.99 – direct from publisher; printed books and eBooks available at *www.Amazon.com*; *www.BN.com*; *www.deepershopping.com*, and wherever books are sold.)

No Worries - Spiritual and Mental Health Counseling for Anxiety, by Elaine Leong Eng, MD – Offering a unique spiritual and mental health perspective on a major malady of our age, this practicing Christian psychiatrist has packed a dose of reality mixed with medicine and faith into a book aimed at informing, inspiring, and equipping those who wish to better help those who struggle with anxiety and related disorders, both inside and outside the church. As one endorser said, "I travel all over the world. I see fellow believers suffering from different forms of anxiety and worry. Dr. Eng's book gives me tools to recognize when people are suffering and how to encourage them to get the help they need." (Printed book: $19.99; PDF eBook: $9.99; both together: $24.99 – direct from publisher; printed books and eBooks available at *www.Amazon.com*; *www.BN.com*; *www.deepershopping.com*, and wherever books are sold.)

If God Is So Good, Why Do I Hurt So Bad?, by David B. Biebel, DMin – This **25th Anniversary Edition** of a best-selling classic (over 200,000 copies in print worldwide, in a dozen languages) is the book's first major revision since its initial release in 1989. This new version features additional original material related to the conundrum of suffering and faith (with principles learned along the way), and chapter ending questions for personal or group use. Endorser Sheila Walsh wrote, "I believe this is one of the most profound, empathetic and beautiful books ever written on the subject of suffering and loss. There is no attempt to quickly ease our pain but rather, with an understanding born in the crucible God uniquely designed for him, David offers a place to stand, a place to fall and a place to rise again. This book left an indelible mark on my heart over twenty years ago and now with this new release the gift is fresh and fragrant. I highly commend this to you!" (Printed book: $14.99; PDF eBook: $9.99; both together: $19.95 – direct from publisher; printed books and eBooks available at *www.Amazon.com*; *www.BN.com*; *www.deepershopping.com*, and wherever books are sold.)

Earlier Releases

We've Got Mail: The New Testament Letters in Modern English – As Relevant Today as Ever! by Rev. Warren C. Biebel, Jr. – A modern English paraphrase of the New Testament Letters, sure to inspire in readers a loving appreciation for God's Word. (Printed book: $9.95; PDF eBook: $6.95; both together: $15.00 – direct from publisher; printed books and eBooks available at *www.Amazon.com*; *www.BN.com*; *www.deepershopping.com*, and wherever books are sold.)

Hearth & Home – Recipes for Life, by Karey Swan (7th Edition) – Far more than a cookbook, this classic is a life book, with recipes for life as well as for great food. Karey describes how to buy and prepare from scratch a wide variety of tantalizing dishes, while weaving into the book's fabric the wisdom of the ages plus the recipe that she and her husband used to raise their kids. A great gift for Christmas or for a new bride. (Perfect Bound book [8 x 10, glossy cover]: $17.95; PDF eBook: $12.95; both together: $24.95 – direct from publisher; printed books and eBooks available at *www.Amazon.com*; *www.BN.com*; *www.deepershopping.com*, and wherever books are sold.)

Who Me, Pray? Prayer 101: Praying Aloud, for Beginners, by Gary A. Burlingame – Who Me, Pray? is a practical guide for prayer, based on Jesus' direction in "The Lord's Prayer," with examples provided for use in typical situations where you might be asked or expected to pray in public. (Printed book: $6.95; PDF eBook: $2.99; both together: $7.95 – direct from publisher; printed books and eBooks available at *www.Amazon.com*; *www.BN.com*; *www.deepershopping.com*, and wherever books are sold.)

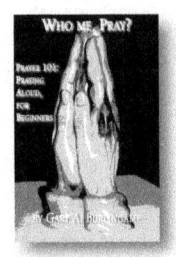

My Broken Heart Sings, the poetry of Gary Burlingame – In 1987, Gary and his wife Debbie lost their son Christopher John, at only six months of age, to a chronic lung disease. This life-changing experience gave them a special heart for helping others through similar loss and pain. (Printed book: $10.95; PDF eBook: $6.95; both together: $13.95 – direct from publisher; printed books and eBooks available at *www.Amazon.com*; *www. BN.com*; *www.deepershopping.com*, and wherever books are sold.)

After Normal: One Teen's Journey Following Her Brother's Death, by Diane Aggen – Based on a journal the author kept following her younger brother's death. It offers helpful insights and understanding for teens facing a similar loss or for those who might wish to understand and help teens facing a similar loss. (Printed book: $11.95; PDF eBook: $6.95; both together: $15.00 – direct from publisher; printed books and eBooks

available at *www.Amazon.com*; *www.BN.com*; *www.deepershopping.com*, and wherever books are sold.)

In the Unlikely Event of a Water Landing – Lessons Learned from Landing in the Hudson River, by Andrew Jamison, MD – The author was flying standby on US Airways Flight 1549 toward Charlotte on January 15, 2009, from New York City, where he had been interviewing for a residency position. Little did he know that the next stop would be the Hudson River. Riveting and inspirational, this book would be especially helpful for people in need of hope and encouragement. (Printed book: $8.95; PDF eBook: $6.95; both together: $12.95 – direct from publisher; printed books and eBooks available at *www.Amazon.com*; *www.BN.com*; *www.deepershopping.com*, and wherever books are sold.)

Finding Martians in the Dark – Everything I Needed to Know About Teaching Took Me Only 30 Years to Learn, by Dan M. Biebel – Packed with wise advice based on hard experience, and laced with humor, this book is a perfect teacher's gift year-round. Susan J. Wegmann, PhD, says, "Biebel's sardonic wit is mellowed by a genuine love for kids and teaching. . . . A Whitman-like sensibility flows through his stories of teaching, learning, and life."

(Printed book: $10.95; PDF eBook: $6.95; Together: $15.00 – direct from publisher; printed books and eBooks available at *www.Amazon.com*; *www.BN.com*; *www.deepershopping.com*, and wherever books are sold.)

Because We're Family and **Because We're Friends,** by Gary A. Burlingame – Sometimes things related to faith can be hard to discuss with your family and friends. These booklets are designed to be given as gifts, to help you open the door to discussing spiritual matters with family members and friends who are open to such a conversation. (Printed book: $5.95 each; PDF eBook: $4.95 each; both together: $9.95 [printed & eBook of the same title] – direct from publisher; printed books and eBooks available at *www.Amazon.com*; *www.BN.com*; *www.deepershopping.com*, and wherever books are sold.)

The Transforming Power of Story: How Telling Your Story Brings Hope to Others and Healing to Yourself, by Elaine Leong Eng, MD, and David B. Biebel, DMin – This book demonstrates, through multiple true life stories, how sharing one's story, especially in a group setting, can bring hope to listeners and healing to the one who shares. Individuals facing difficulties will find this book greatly encouraging. (Printed book: $14.99; PDF eBook: $9.99; both together: $19.99 – direct from publisher; printed books and eBooks available at *www.Amazon.com*; *www.BN.com*; *www.deepershopping.com*, and wherever books are sold.)

You Deserved a Better Father: Good Parenting Takes a Plan, by Robb Brandt, MD – About parenting by intention, and other lessons the author learned through the loss of his firstborn son. It is especially for parents who believe that bits and pieces of leftover time will be enough for their own children. (Printed book: $12.95 each; PDF eBook: $6.95; both together: $17.95 – direct from publisher; printed books and eBooks available at

www.Amazon.com; *www.BN.com*; *www.deepershopping.com*, and wherever books are sold.)

Printed Cover   eBook Cover

Jonathan, You Left Too Soon, by David B. Biebel, DMin – One pastor's journey through the loss of his son, into the darkness of depression, and back into the light of joy again, emerging with a renewed sense of mission. (Printed book: $12.95; PDF eBook: $5.99; both together: $15.00 – direct from publisher; printed books and eBooks available at *www.Amazon.com*; *www.BN.com*; *www.deepershopping.com*, and wherever books are sold.)

Unless otherwise noted on the site itself, shipping is free for all products purchased through www.healthylifepress.com.

The Spiritual Fitness Checkup for the 50-Something Woman, by Sharon V. King, PhD – Following the stages of a routine medical exam, the author describes ten spiritual fitness "checkups" midlife women can conduct to assess their spiritual health and tone up their relationship with God. Each checkup consists of the author's personal reflections, a Scripture reference for meditation, and a "Spiritual Pulse Check," with exercises readers can use for personal application. (Printed book: $8.95; PDF eBook: $6.95; both together: $12.95 – direct from publisher; printed books and eBooks available at www.Amazon.com; www.BN.com; www.deepershopping.com, and wherever books are sold.)

The Other Side of Life – Over 60? God Still Has a Plan for You, by Rev. Warren C. Biebel, Jr. – Drawing on biblical examples and his 60-plus years of pastoral experience, Rev. Biebel helps older (and younger) adults understand God's view of aging and the rich life available to everyone who seeks a deeper relationship with God as they age. Rev. Biebel explains how to: Identify God's ongoing plan for your life; Rely on faith to manage the anxieties of aging;

Form positive, supportive relationships; Cultivate patience; Cope with new technologies; Develop spiritual integrity; Understand the effects of dementia; Develop a Christ-centered perspective of aging. (Printed book: $10.95; PDF eBook: $6.95; both together: $15.00 – direct from publisher; printed books and eBooks available at www.Amazon.com; www.BN.com; www.deepershopping.com, and wherever books are sold.)

My Faith, My Poetry, by Gary A. Burlingame – This unique book of Christian poetry is actually two in one. The first collection of poems, A Day in the Life, explores a working parent's daily journey of faith. The reader is carried from morning to bedtime, from "In the Details," to "I Forgot to Pray," back to "Home Base," and finally to "Eternal Love Divine." The second collection of poems, Come Running, is wonder, joy, and faith wrapped up in words that encourage and inspire the mind and the heart. (Printed book: $10.95; PDF eBook: $6.95; both together: $13.95 – direct from publisher; printed books and eBooks available at www.Amazon.com; www.BN.com; www.deepershopping.com, and wherever books are sold.)

On Eagles' Wings, by Sara Eggleston – One woman's life journey from idyllic through chaotic to joy, carried all the way by the One who has promised to never leave us nor forsake us. Remarkable, poignant, moving, and inspiring, this autobiographical account will help many who are facing difficulties that seem too great to overcome or even bear at all. It is proof that Isaiah 40:31 is as true today as when it was penned, "But they that wait upon the LORD shall renew their strength; they shall mount up with wings as eagles; they shall run, and not be weary; and they shall walk, and not faint." (Printed book: $14.95; PDF eBook: $8.95; both together: $22.95 – direct from publisher; printed books and eBooks available at *www.Amazon.com*; *www.BN.com*; *www.deepershopping.com*, and wherever books are sold.)

Richer Descriptions, by Gary A. Burlingame – A unique and handy manual, covering all nine human senses in seven chapters, for Christian speakers and writers. Exercises and a speaker's checklist equip speakers to engage their audiences in a richer experience. Writing examples and a writer's guide help writers bring more life to the characters and scenes of their stories. Bible references encourage a deeper appreciation of being created by God for a sensory existence. (Printed book: $15.95; PDF eBook: $8.95; both together: $22.95 – direct from publisher; printed books and eBooks available at *www.Amazon.com*; *www.BN.com*; *www.deepershopping.com*, and wherever books are sold.)

Treasuring Grace, by Rob Plumley and Tracy Roberts – This novel was inspired by a dream. Liz Swanson's life isn't quite what she'd imagined, but she considers herself lucky. She has a good husband, beautiful children, and fulfillment outside of her home through volunteer work. On some days she doesn't even notice the dull ache in her heart. While she's preparing for their summer kickoff at Lake George, the ache disappears and her sudden happiness is mistaken for anticipation of their weekend. However, as the family heads north, there are clouds on the horizon that have nothing to do with the weather. Only Liz's daughter, who's found some of her mother's hidden journals, has any idea what's wrong. But by the end of the weekend, there will be no escaping the truth or its painful buried secrets.

(Printed: $12.95; PDF eBook: $7.95; both together: $19.95 – direct from publisher; printed books and eBooks available at *www.Amazon.com*; *www.BN.com*; *www.deepershopping.com*, and wherever books are sold.)

From Orphan to Physician – The Winding Path, by Chun-Wai Chan, MD – From the foreword: "In this book, Dr. Chan describes how his family escaped to Hong Kong, how they survived in utter poverty, and how he went from being an orphan to graduating from Harvard Medical School and becoming a cardiologist. The writing is fluent, easy to read and understand. The sequence of events is realistic, emotionally moving, spiritually touching, heartwarming, and thought provoking. The book illustrates . . . how one must have faith in order to walk through life's winding path." (Printed book: $14.95; PDF eBook: $8.95; both together: $22.95 – direct from publisher; printed books and eBooks available at *www.Amazon.com*; *www.BN.com*; *www.deepershopping.com*, and wherever books are sold.)

12 Parables, by Wayne Faust – Timeless Christian stories about doubt, fear, change, grief, and more. Using tight, entertaining prose, professional musician and comedy performer Wayne Faust manages to deal with difficult concepts in a simple, straightforward way. These are stories you can read aloud over and over—to your spouse, your family, or in a group setting. Packed with emotion and just enough mystery to keep you wondering, while providing lots of points to ponder and discuss when you're through, these stories relate the gospel in the tradition of the greatest speaker of parables the world has ever known, who appears in them often. (Printed book: $14.95; PDF eBook: $8.95; both together: $22.95 – direct from publisher; printed books and eBooks available at *www.Amazon.com*; *www.BN.com*; *www.deepershopping.com*, and wherever books are sold.)

The Answer is Always "Jesus," by Aram Haroutunian, who gave children's sermons for 15 years at a large church in Golden, Colorado—well over 500 in all. This book contains 74 of his most unforgettable presentations—due to the children's responses. Pastors, homeschoolers, parents who often lead family devotions, or other storytellers will find these stories, along with comments about props and how to prepare and present them, an invaluable asset in reconnecting with the simplest, most profound truths of Scripture, and then to envision how best to communicate these so even a child can understand them. (Printed book: $12.95; PDF eBook: $8.95; both together: $19.95 – direct from publisher; printed books and eBooks available at *www.Amazon.com*; *www.BN.com*; *www.deepershopping.com*, and wherever books are sold.)

Handbook of Faith, by Rev. Warren C. Biebel, Jr. – The New York Times World 2011 Almanac claimed that there are 2 billion, 200 thousand Christians in the world, with "Christians" being defined as "followers of Christ." The original 12 followers of Christ changed the world; indeed, they changed the history of the world. So this author, a pastor with over 60 years' experience, poses and answers this logical question: "If there are so many 'Christians' on this planet, why are they so relatively ineffective in serving the One they claim to follow?" Answer: Because, unlike Him, they do not know and trust the Scriptures, implicitly. This little volume will help you do that. (Printed book: $8.95; PDF eBook: $6.95; both together: $13.95 – direct from publisher; printed books and eBooks available at *www.Amazon.com*; *www.BN.com*; *www.deepershopping.com*, and wherever books are sold.)

Pieces of My Heart, by David L. Wood – Eighty-two lessons from normal everyday life. David's hope is that these stories will spark thoughts about God's constant involvement and intervention in our lives and stir a sense of how much He cares about every detail that is important to us. The piece missing represents his son, Daniel, who died in a fire shortly before his first birthday. (Printed book: $16.95; PDF eBook: $8.95; both together: $24.95 – direct from publisher; printed books and eBooks available at *www.Amazon.com*; *www.BN.com*; *www.deepershopping.com*, and wherever books are sold.)

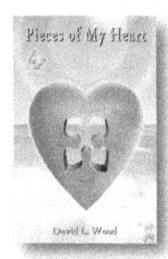

Unless otherwise noted on the site itself, shipping is free for all products purchased through www.healthylifepress.com.

 **Dream House,** by Justa Carpenter – Written by a New England builder of several hundred homes, the idea for this book came to him one day as he was driving that came to him one day as was driving from one job site to another. He pulled over and recorded it so he would remember it, and now you will remember it, too, if you believe, as he does, that ". . . He who has begun a good work in you will complete it until the day of Jesus Christ." (Printed book: $10.95; PDF eBook: $6.95; both together: $13.95 – direct from publisher; printed books and eBooks available at *www.Amazon.com*; *www.BN.com*; *www.deepershopping.com*, and wherever books are sold.)

A Simply Homemade Clean, by homesteader Lisa Barthuly – "Somewhere along the path, it seems we've lost our gumption, the desire to make things ourselves," says the author. "Gone are the days of 'do it yourself.' Really . . . why bother? There are a slew of retailers just waiting for us with anything and everything we could need; packaged up all pretty, with no thought or effort required. It is the manifestation of 'progress' . . . right?" I don't buy  that!" Instead, Lisa describes how to make safe and effective cleansers for home, laundry, and body right in your own home. This saves money and avoids exposure to harmful chemicals often found in commercially produced cleansers. (**Full-color** printed book: $16.99; PDF eBook: $6.95; both together: $22.95 – direct from publisher; printed books and eBooks available at *www.Amazon.com*; *www.BN.com*; *www.deepershopping.com*, and wherever books are sold.)

 **The Secret of Singing Springs,** by Monte Swan – One Colorado family's treasure-hunting adventure along the trail of Jesse James. The Secret of Singing Springs is written to capture for children and their parents the spirit of the hunt—the hunt for treasure as in God's Truth, which is the objective of walking the Way of Wisdom that is described in Proverbs. (Printed book: $12.95, PDF eBook: $9.99; both together: $19.99 – direct from publisher; printed books and eBooks available at *www.Amazon.com*; *www.BN.com*; *www.deepershopping.com*, and wherever books are sold.)

God Loves You Circle, by Michelle Johnson – Daily inspiration for your deeper walk with Christ. This collection of short stories of Christian living will make you laugh, make you cry, but most of all make you contemplate—the meaning and value of walking with the Master moment-by-moment, day-by-day. (**Full-color** printed book: $17.95; PDF eBook: $9.99; both together: $22.99 – direct from publisher; printed books and eBooks available at www.Amazon.com; www.BN.com; www.deepershopping.com, and wherever books are sold.)

Our God-Given Senses, by Gary A. Burlingame – Did you know humans have NINE senses? The Bible draws on these senses to reveal spiritual truth. We are to taste and see that the Lord is a good. We are to carry the fragrance of Christ. Our faith is produced upon hearing. Jesus asked Thomas to touch him. God created us for a sensory experience and that is what you will find in this book. (Printed book: $12.99; PDF eBook: $9.99; both together: $19.99 – direct  from publisher; printed books and eBooks available at www.Amazon.com; www.BN.com; www.deepershopping.com, and wherever books are sold.)

Vows, a Romantic novel by F. F. Whitestone – When the police cruiser pulled up to the curb outside, Faith Framingham's heart skipped a beat, for she could see that Chuck, who should have been driving, was not in the vehicle. Chuck's partner, Sandy, stepped out slowly. Sandy's pursed lips and ashen face spoke volumes. Faith waited by the front door, her hands clasped tightly, to counter the fact that her mind was already reeling. "Love never fails." A compelling story. (Printed book: $12.99; PDF eBook: $9.99; both together, $19.99 – direct from publisher; printed books and eBooks available at www.Amazon.com; www.BN.com; www.deepershopping.com, and wherever books are sold.)

Unless otherwise noted on the site itself, shipping is free for all products purchased through www.healthylifepress.com.

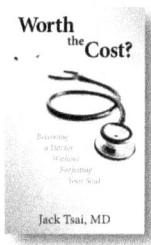

Worth the Cost?, by Jack Tsai, MD – The author was happily on his way to obtaining the American Dream until he decided to take seriously Jesus' command, "Come, follow me." Join him as he explores the cost of medical education and Christian discipleship. Planning to serve God in your future vocation? Take care that your desires do not get side-tracked by the false promises of this world. What you should be doing now so when you are done with your training you will still want to serve God. (Printed book: $12.99, PDF eBook: $9.99; both together: $19.99 – direct from publisher; printed books and eBooks available at *www.Amazon.com*; *www.BN.com*; *www.deepershopping.com*, and wherever books are sold.)

Nature: God's Second Book – An Essential Link to Restoring Your Personal Health and Wellness: Body, Mind, and Spirit, by Elvy P. Rolle – An inspirational book that looks at nature across the seasons of nature and of life. It uses the biblical Emmaus Journey as an analogy for life's journey, and offers ideas for using nature appreciation and exploration to reduce life's stresses. The author shares her personal story of how she came to grips with this concept after three trips to the emergency room. (**Full-color** printed book: $12.99; PDF eBook $8.99; both together: $16.99 – direct from publisher; printed books and eBooks available at *www.Amazon.com*; *www.BN.com*; *www.deepershopping.com*, and wherever books are sold.)

He Waited, by LaDonna Cooper – Inspires readers to wait upon the Lord for His best for them; stresses the importance of putting God's purpose above one's own; emphasizes that God's love is unconditional; demonstrates the wisdom of waiting, through a combination of positive insights, encouragement, biblical examples and principles. Decorated with original poetry by the author. For singles and others who are waiting. Distributed primarily through *www.Amazon.com*. (Printed book: $10.99; PDF eBook: $9.99; both together: $15.99 – direct from publisher; printed books and eBooks available at *www.Amazon.com*; *www.BN.com*; *www.deepershopping.com*, and wherever books are sold.)

Seasonal

 **The Big Black Book – What the Christmas Tree Saw,** by Rev. Warren C. Biebel, Jr. – An original Christmas story, from the perspective of the Christmas tree. This little book is especially suitable for parents to read to their children at Christmas time or all year-round. (**Full-color** printed book: $9.95; PDF eBook: $4.95; both together: $12.95 – direct from publisher; printed books and eBooks available at *www.Amazon.com*; *www.BN.com*; *www.deepershopping.com*, and wherever books are sold.)

About Healthy Life Press

Healthy Life Press was founded with a primary goal of helping previously unpublished authors to get their works to market, and to reissue worthy, previously published works that were no longer available. Our mission is to help people toward optimal vitality by providing resources promoting physical, emotional, spiritual, and relational health as viewed from a Christian perspective. We see health as a verb, and achieving optimal health as a process—a crucial process for followers of Christ if we are to love the Lord with all our heart, soul, mind, AND strength, and our neighbors as ourselves—for as long as He leaves us here. We are a collaborative and cooperative small Christian publisher. We share costs/we share proceeds.

For information about publishing with us, e-mail: <u>healthylifepress@aol.com</u>.